Contents

Basic Counselling Skills

A HELPER'S MANUAL

Richard Nelson-Jones

SAGE Publications
London · Thousand Oaks · New Delhi

© Richard Nelson-Jones 2003

First published 2003

Apart from any fair dealing for the purposes of research or
private study, or criticism or review, as permitted under the
Copyright, Designs and Patents Act, 1988, this publication
may be reproduced, stored or transmitted in any form, or by
any means, only with the prior permission in writing of the
publishers, or in the case of reprographic reproduction, in
accordance with the terms of licences issued by the
Copyright Licensing Agency. Inquiries concerning
reproduction outside those terms should be
sent to the publishers.

 SAGE Publications Ltd
6 Bonhill Street
London EC2A 4PU

SAGE Publications Inc
2455 Teller Road
Thousand Oaks, California 91320

SAGE Publications India Pvt Ltd
32, M-Block Market
Greater Kailash – I
New Delhi 110 048

British Library Cataloguing in Publication data

A catalogue record for this book is
available from the British Library

ISBN 0 7619 4960 7
ISBN 0 7619 4961 5 (pbk)

Library of Congress Control Number: 2002102288

Typeset by M Rules
Printed in Great Britain by
TJ International, Padstow, Cornwall

Preface

Welcome to *Basic Counselling Skills: A Helper's Manual*. Those using counselling skills can be divided into two groups: professionally accredited counsellors/psychotherapists and helpers. Helpers are all those people who use counselling skills as paraprofessional or quasi-counsellors, as part of non-counselling primary work roles, as volunteers in counselling and helping agencies or in peer support groups. The prime purpose of this book is to support the training and practice of such helpers. In addition, this book may be used as an introduction to counselling skills for those intending to become professional counsellors.

I designed this book in response to the question 'How can I make this book as easy to access and learn from as possible?' My solution was to divide the book into 28 brief chapters or learning units and to restrict myself to essential content only. I do not provide references throughout the text, since this book is intended for the practitioner rather than for an academic audience.

The book is divided into three parts. *Part I, Introduction,* consists of 6 chapters that lay the groundwork for understanding the use of basic counselling skills across a range of settings. *Part II, Specific counselling skills,* consists of 18 chapters designed to introduce a wide range of basic counselling skills. Each chapter describes the skill, provides one or more examples of its use, and then encourages the reader to practice the skill by undertaking one or more activities. *Part III, Further considerations,* consists of 4 chapters that aim to raise readers' awareness of dealing with clients from different backgrounds, ethical and supervision issues, and how to become more skilled. In addition, I provide an extensive Annotated Bibliography.

This preface is concise and to the point. I hope readers will find all 28 chapters of this book similarly honed and focused. Good luck and good skills.

Richard Nelson-Jones

PART I

Introduction

1 Who are counsellors and helpers?

Below are concerns that people might wish to share with another.

'I'm feeling depressed and lonely.'
'I'm very anxious about my forthcoming exams.'
'There is a problem between me and the wife and I just don't know what to do about it.'
'My boss tells me that if I can't control my temper, I could lose my job.'
'I've just had a heart attack and want to learn to live more sensibly.'
'I'm growing old and frail and am afraid of dying.'
'I feel that I am being sexually harassed at work.'
'I've just lost my job and feel dreadful about my prospects.'
'I'm experiencing difficulty settling in to a new culture.'

There are six main categories of people who might offer help with such concerns. First, there are professional counsellors and psychotherapists. Such counselling and therapy professionals, who have undergone training on appropriately accredited courses, include clinical psychologists, counselling psychologists, psychotherapists, counsellors and some psychiatrists and social workers. Second, there are paraprofessional or quasi-counsellors, who may have considerable training in counselling yet are not accredited as counselling professionals. Third, there are those who use counselling and helping skills as part of their work. Here the primary focus of the work may be teaching, managing, supervising or providing religious, social work, medical, financial, legal and trade union services. These jobs require people to use counselling skills some of the time if they are to be maximally effective. Fourth, there are voluntary counsellors and helpers. Volunteers usually receive training in counselling skills. They may work in settings like youth counselling services and in numerous voluntary agencies that provide invaluable services, such as the Samaritans. Fifth, there are people who are part of peer helping or support networks of varying degrees of formality. Such peer support networks frequently cover areas of diversity such as culture, race, sexual orientation, and support for women and for men. Last, there are informal helpers. All of us have the opportunity to assist others, be it in the role of marital partner, parent, friend, relative or work colleague.

In the above paragraph, as is still often the case in everyday parlance, I used the terms 'counsellors' and 'helpers' as though they were interchangeable. However, this blurring is likely to become increasingly unhelpful as the counselling and psychotherapy profession becomes more established and regulated. I now clarify some differences between counsellors and helpers.

Who are counsellors?

Here I will group as counsellors all those who are professionally trained and accredited to conduct counselling and psychotherapy. Therapy is derived from the Greek work 'therapeia' meaning healing. Attempts to differentiate between counselling and psychotherapy are never wholly successful. Because counselling and psychotherapy represent diverse rather than uniform knowledge and activities, it is more helpful to think of counselling *approaches* and psychological or 'talking' *therapies*.

Possible ways of attempting to distinguish counselling from psychotherapy include the fact that psychotherapy deals more with mental disorders than counselling, that psychotherapy is longer-term and deeper, and that psychotherapy is predominantly associated with medical settings. However, matters are by no means this clear-cut. Many counsellors work in medical settings, have clients with recognised mental disorders and do longer-term work that may or may not be of a psychodynamic nature.

There is huge overlap between counselling and psychotherapy. As an illustration of this overlap, the Psychotherapy and Counselling Federation of Australia (PACFA) promulgates 'A definition of counselling and psychotherapy' as a single statement. Both counselling and psychotherapy are psychological processes that use the same theoretical models. Each stresses the need to value the client as a person, to listen carefully and sympathetically to what they have to say, and to foster the capacity for self-help and personal responsibility. For the purposes of this book, the terms 'counselling' and 'psychotherapy' are used interchangeably. Box 1.1 profiles three examples of counselling and psychotherapy professionals.

Box 1.1 Examples of professional counsellors and psychotherapists

Jamie, 53, is an accredited psychotherapist in private practice. His caseload is partly composed of adult clients who come to his consulting rooms and partly made up of staff he counsels on the premises of an oil company where he works as a sessional psychologist. In addition, Jamie leads some private counselling groups focused on helping couples improve their relationships.

Meredith, 44, is an accredited counselling psychologist who specializes in working with people with health concerns, for example pain management and preventing further heart attacks. Though some of her clients come to see her privately, she mostly works in a primary care setting as part of a healthcare team.

Susan, 33, is an accredited student counsellor in a college setting. Though most of her clients are students, she also has some clients drawn from the academic and non-academic staff at her institution. In addition to individual work, Susan leads training groups for students in such areas as study skills, assertion skills and managing conflict skills. Susan is studying for a doctorate in counselling and ultimately would like to become a counsellor trainer.

What constitutes professional training as a counsellor? Though subject to change, the following gives the reader some idea of what is required. Courses recognized by the British Association for Counselling and Psychotherapy (BACP) are required to have a minimum of 400 hours staff/student contact time, with students undertaking a minimum of 100 hours of supervised counselling practice. Such courses can be of one year full-time duration or spread over three or four years part-time. For those wishing to train as psychotherapists, training offered by organizational members of the United Kingdom Council for Psychotherapy (UKCP) is not normally shorter than four years part-time duration. Such training involves supervized clinical work and usually personal therapy in the model being taught. In Australia,

PACFA requires courses run by its member associations to consist of a minimum 250 hours of training and supervision. Regarding professional qualifications, two further points are worthy of mention. First, a number of people, such as some social workers and nurses, combine professional qualifications in their primary role with professional qualifications in counselling and psychotherapy. Second, completion of an approved course of counselling or psychotherapy training can no longer be equated with accreditation, since increasingly professional counsellors and psychotherapists are required to undertake mandatory continuing professional development (CPD) requirements by their professional associations.

Who are helpers?

Sometimes, as in the case of Gerard Egan's textbook *The Skilled Helper*, the term 'helper' is used as a generic term to cover all those engaged in using counselling and helping skills, be they counselling and psychotherapy professionals or otherwise. Here, I am using the term helper in a more restricted sense to include paraprofessional or quasi-counsellors, those who use counselling skills as part of other primary roles, those engaged in voluntary counselling and helping, and those who participate in peer helping or support networks.

Paraprofessional counsellors are trained in counselling skills, but at a level that falls short of professional counselling or psychotherapy accreditation. For example, some nurses have attended a number of counselling courses and may be skilled at dealing with the problems of specific categories of patients. People with such backgrounds might be called counsellors in their work settings, for example nurse counsellors. However, if the term 'counsellor' in a given context is limited only to those with recognized professional qualifications and accreditation in the area, paraprofessional counsellors become categorized as helpers, despite the quality of their skills.

Box 1.2 provides some examples of helpers, who are not paraprofessional counsellors yet who are using counselling skills either as part of their work, in voluntary settings or on a peer support basis. The examples in Box 1.2 are only illustrative of the vast range of people who use counselling skills when performing helping roles.

Box 1.2   Examples of helpers using counselling skills

Emily, 38, is a teacher in a large mixed secondary school. She has been allocated time in her schedule to act as careers advisor for a group of students, some of whom have little idea about whether they wish to continue their education and what they want to do with their lives.

Tina, 24, meets regularly with Laura, 29, as part of a women's support network. Tina and Laura engage in co-helping in which, whenever they meet, they share the time between them so that each has a turn to be in the client and helper roles.

Leslie, 25, works as a volunteer in a programme designed to support people with AIDS and their partners. After some initial training in counselling and caring skills, Leslie regularly visits the homes of those to whom he has been assigned as a helper.

Rajiv, 30, is a community and youth worker in an inner city area. His duties involve liaising with the south Asian migrant community in his local council's jurisdiction and helping them and their children with their practical and emotional problems, including coping with racist incidents.

Chris, 44, is an Anglican priest in a country town. He finds that he uses counselling skills in both the spiritual guidance and the practical dimensions of his pastoral work. In addition, Chris uses counselling skills when preparing couples for marriage within a Christian context.

Helen, 37, works as a counsellor in a pregnancy advisory service where individuals and couples consult her about birth control information and decisions. Helen finds it important to use counselling skills since contraception is a very sensitive topic for some clients to discuss.

Sally, 42, is a probation and parole officer who uses counselling skills to build trust with her clients and to help them with their practical and emotional problems. Many clients find the support that Sally provides is invaluable in helping them stay out of trouble and reintegrate into society.

Let's take a further look at some ways in which helpers can be distinguished from professional counsellors and psychotherapists. So far two main distinguishing areas have been identified. Helpers perform different *roles* to those of counsellors and psychotherapists. Counsellors have as their primary role conducting counselling, whether this be individual, couples, group or family counselling. Helpers often either have their primary role in another area or are using helping skills in voluntary and peer support capacities. Related to different roles, helpers differ from counsellors in their *training*. Counsellors are primarily trained to counsel, whereas helpers may be primarily trained to be social workers, nurses, probation officers, priests, welfare workers, managers and in a host of other occupations. Furthermore, voluntary workers usually have primary work roles in non-counselling occupations, for which they have likely received the bulk of their training.

The *goals* of helping can both overlap with yet differ from those of counselling. The primary purpose of counselling and psychotherapy is to help clients address psychological issues in their lives, for example, becoming less depressed or anxious, and to work through decisions and crises that have a distinct psychological dimension to them. Sometimes such psychological issues are central to helping. On other occasions, helpers use counselling skills to assist people to deal with goals where the overt psychological dimensions appear secondary, if not irrelevant, to the recipients of the services. There are many examples of this in Box 1.2; for instance, receiving pregnancy advice and probation and parole support.

The *settings* or contexts for helping can differ from those for counselling. Most often counselling takes place in offices, be they private or institutional, set aside specially for that activity. The décor of such offices is designed to support the purpose of counselling, for instance, functional easy chairs with a coffee table between them. Often counselling services are located in specially designated areas, for instance, student counselling services. Helpers may sometimes use counselling skills in areas designed for counselling, for instance, in some voluntary agencies. However, frequently helpers use counselling skills in locations that represent their primary work role. Such locations include personnel offices, classrooms, tutorial rooms, hospital wards, outplacement clinics, churches, banks, law offices and community centres. Furthermore, while counsellors rarely go outside formal locations, helpers such as priests, nurses, social workers and members of peer support networks may use counselling skills in people's home settings.

A further distinction is that the *relationship* in which helpers use counselling skills often differs from the more formal counselling relationship, which is likely to have clear boundaries structured around the respective tasks of counsellor and client. Sometimes helping relationships may have similarly clear helper–client boundaries, though the prime agenda may or may not be psychological counselling. Frequently, however, helping relationships take place in the context of other relationships, such as teacher–student, priest–parishioner, line manager–worker, social worker–client, nurse or doctor–patient. Whereas dual relationships, in which counsellors perform more than one role in relation to clients, are frowned upon in counselling, they may be built into the fabric of many helping relationships. Furthermore, as mentioned above, sometimes helping relationships include home visits.

Helpers and clients

For the purposes of this book, the term 'helper' is used to refer to all those people who use counselling skills either as paraprofessional or quasi-counsellors, as part of non-counselling primary work roles, as volunteers in counselling and helping agencies, or in peer support networks. Though some such helpers might nevertheless be called counsellors, the term 'counsellor' in this book is reserved for professionally trained and accredited counsellors and psychotherapists.

The term 'client' is used as a shorthand way to describe the numerous people with whom helpers interact when they use counselling skills. Some such people may already be referred to as clients. However, just as helpers do not have their primary role as counsellors, their clients too may have other primary roles such as pupils, students, customers, patients, local residents, young people, old people and peers.

2 What are basic counselling skills?

What is a counselling skill? One application of the word 'skill' pertains to *areas* of skill: for instance, listening skills or disclosing skills. Another application refers to *level of competence*, for instance, skilled or unskilled in a particular area. However, competence in a skill is best viewed not as an either/or matter in which helpers either possess or do not possess a skill, but rather, within a skills area, it is preferable to think of helpers as possessing good skills or poor skills or a mixture of the two. In all skills areas helpers are likely to possess mixtures of strengths and weaknesses. For instance, in the skills area of listening, helpers may be good at understanding clients but poor at showing their understanding. Similarly, in just about all areas of their functioning, clients will possess a mixture of poor and good skills.

A third application of the word 'skill' relates to the *knowledge and sequence of choices* entailed in implementing a given skill. The essential element of any skill is the ability to make and implement sequences of choices to achieve objectives. For instance, if helpers are to be good at listening deeply and accurately to clients, they have to make and implement effective choices in this skills area. The object of counselling skills training and supervision is to help students, in the skills areas targeted by their training programmes, to move more in the direction of making good rather than poor choices. For example, in the skills area of active listening the objective would be to enable students to make good choices in the process not only of understanding clients but also in showing that understanding to them.

When thinking of any area of helper or client communication, there are two main considerations: first, what are the components of skilled

external behaviour and, second, what interferes with or enhances enacting that behaviour. Thus a counselling skill like active listening consists
both of skilled interpersonal communication and skilled intrapersonal
mental processing. One approach to understanding this is to acknowledge that outer behaviour originates in the mind and that, as a
consequence, both thinking and behaviour are fundamentally mental
processes. Though I distinguish between communication and/or action
skills and mind skills, the distinction is somewhat artificial since external communication as well as internal thoughts are created in the mind.

There are two main categories of helper and client skills. First, there
are communication and action skills, or skills that entail external behaviour. Second, there are mind skills, or skills that entail internal
behaviour. Readers may wonder why I do not talk about feelings skills
and physical reactions skills. The reason for this is that feelings and
physical reactions are essentially part of people's instinctual or animal
nature and are not skills in themselves. However, helpers and clients
can influence how they feel and physically react by how they
communicate/act and think.

Communication and action skills

Communication and action skills involve observable behaviours. They
are what people do and how they do it, rather than what and how
they feel and think. For instance, it is one thing for helpers to feel concern for clients, and another to act on this feeling. How do helpers
communicate to clients and act to show their sympathy and compassion for them? They need to do so with their words, voices and body
language. Communication and action skills vary by area of application:
for instance, listening skills, questioning skills and challenging skills.
Box 2.1 presents the five main ways in which helpers and clients can
send communication and action skills messages.

Mind skills

In the last 20 to 30 years, there has been a major trend in counselling
and psychotherapy towards trying to change clients' self-defeating
thoughts and mental processes as a way of helping them to feel and act
better. These approaches are known as the cognitive therapies. The
same insights can be applied to the thoughts and mental processes of
helping students and helpers as they both learn and use counselling
skills.

Box 2.1 Five main ways of sending communication/action skills messages

Verbal messages Messages that people send with words.

Vocal messages Messages that people send through their voices: for example, through volume, articulation, pitch, emphasis and speech rate.

Body messages Messages that people send with their bodies: for instance, through gaze, eye contact, facial expression, posture, gestures, physical proximity and clothes and grooming.

Touch messages A special category of body messages. Messages that people send with touch through the parts of body that they use, what parts of another's body they touch, how gentle or firm they are, and whether or not they have permission.

Action-taking messages Messages that people send when they are not face-to-face with clients, for example sending letters, e-mails or invoices.

Helpers can learn counselling skills and assist clients much more effectively if they harness their mind's potential. How can helpers control their thoughts so that they can beneficially influence how they communicate? First, they can understand that they have a mind with a capacity for super-conscious thinking – or thinking about thinking – that they can develop. Second, they can become much more efficient in thinking about their thinking if they view their mental processes in terms of skills that they can train themselves to exercise and control. Third, in daily life as well as in their counselling skills training, they can assiduously practice using their mind skills to influence their communication.

Counselling skills involve mental processing both to guide external behaviour and to ensure thinking that supports rather than undermines skilled external communication. Let's take the skill of active listening. To some extent it is easy to describe the central elements of the external communication involved. On paper, these external communication skills may appear straightforward. However, most counselling skills students and many experienced counsellors and helpers struggle to listen well. The question then arises: 'If the external communication skills of listening well are so relatively easy to outline, why don't students and experienced helpers just do them?' The simple answer is that one's mind can both enhance and get in the way of one's external communication. Thus counselling skills are both mind and communication skills.

Box 2.2 provides descriptions of three central mental processes or mind skills. These skills are derived from the work of leading cognitive therapists, such as Aaron Beck and Albert Ellis. Readers may find references to their work in the annotated bibliography. These mind skills are relevant to counselling skills students, helpers and clients alike. The contents of Chapters 19, 20 and 21 of this book, focusing on strategies for changing clients' thinking in these mind skills areas, also apply to changing the thinking of counselling skills students and helpers.

Box 2.2 Three central mind skills

Creating self-talk Instead of talking to themselves negatively before, during and after specific situations, people can acknowledge that they have choices and make coping self-statements that assist them to stay calm and cool, establish their goals, coach them in what to do, and affirm their strengths, skills and support factors. In addition people can use self-talk to create visual images that support their verbal self-statements.

Creating rules People's unrealistic rules make irrational demands on them, others and the environment, for instance, 'I must always be happy', 'Others must look after me' and 'My environment should not contain any suffering'. Instead they can develop realistic or preferential rules: for instance, 'I prefer to be happy much of the time, but it is unrealistic to expect this all the time.'

Creating perceptions People can learn to test the reality of their perceptions rather than jump to conclusions. They can distinguish between fact and inference and make their inferences as accurate as possible.

In reality, the mind skills tend to overlap. For instance, all of the skills involve self-talk. However, here self-talk refers to self-statements relevant to coping with specific situations. Interrelationships between skills can also be viewed on the dimension of depth. Arguably, counsellors or clients who believe in the rule 'I must always be happy' are more prone to perceiving events as negative than those who do not share this rule.

Feelings and physical reactions

To a large extent, people are what they feel. Important feelings include happiness, interest, surprise, fear, sadness, anger and disgust or contempt. Dictionary definitions of feelings tend to use words like 'physical sensation', 'emotions' and 'awareness'. All three of these words illustrate a dimension of feelings. Feelings as *physical sensations* or as *physical reactions* represent people's underlying animal nature. People are animals first, persons second. As such they need to learn to value and live with their underlying animal nature. The word *emotions* implies movement. Feelings are processes. People are subject to a continuous flow of biological experiencing. *Awareness* implies that people can be conscious of their feelings. However, at varying levels and in different ways, they may also be out of touch with them.

Physical reactions both represent and accompany feelings and, in a sense, are indistinguishable. For example, bodily changes associated with anxiety can include galvanic skin response – detectable electrical changes taking place in the skin, raised blood pressure, a pounding heart and a rapid pulse, shallow and rapid breathing, muscular tension, drying of the mouth, stomach problems such as ulcers, speech difficulties such as stammering, sleep difficulties, and sexual problems such as complete or partial loss of desire. Other physical reactions include a slowing down of body movements when depressed and dilated eye pupils in moments of anger or sexual attraction. Sometimes people react to their physical reactions. For example, in anxiety and panic attacks, they may first feel tense and anxious and then become even more tense and anxious because of this initial feeling.

Feelings and physical reactions are central to the helping process. Helpers require the capacity to experience and understand both their own and their clients' feelings. However, just because feelings represent people's animal nature, this does not mean that helpers and their clients can do nothing about them. In helping, three somewhat overlapping areas where feelings and accompanying physical reactions are important, are experiencing feelings, expressing feelings and managing feelings. In each of these three areas, helpers can work with clients' communications/actions and thoughts and mental processes to influence how they feel and physically react.

Basic counselling skills

Let's get down to basics. The word 'basic' when used in conjunction with counselling skills implies a repertoire of central counselling skills on which helpers can base their helping practice. Another related meaning of the term basic is that of being fundamental or primary rather than advanced. The quality of the helper–client relationship is essential to successful helping encounters. Consequently, many basic skills are those that will enhance how well helpers and clients connect with one another. Such skills include understanding the client's internal frame of reference and reflecting their feelings. Other basic skills entail helping clients to understand their problems and situations more clearly, for example, helpers can ask key questions about clients' feelings, physical reactions, thoughts, communications and actions. Still other basic skills can focus on simple and straightforward ways of assisting clients to change how they think, feel, communicate and act. All helpers require basic counselling skills for relating to clients and for helping them to understand their concerns. The extent and ways in which helpers extend their repertoire of basic counselling skills to include skills for assisting client change is likely to be much more a matter of what each individual finds useful.

3 Approaches to counselling and helping

This chapter draws readers' attention to the fact that there are different theoretical approaches that underpin counselling. Though not the focus of this book, understanding theory can also be relevant to helpers who, while not conducting formal counselling, nevertheless seek reasoned explanations for their clients' and their own behaviour. In this chapter I use the term 'theories of counselling and helping' to indicate that these theories are relevant to formal counselling and also to less formal ways of helping clients. Theories of counselling and helping are conceptual frameworks that allow practitioners to think systematically about human development and the counselling and helping process.

Counselling and helping theories may be viewed as possessing four main dimensions if they are to be stated adequately:

1 a statement of the basic concepts or assumptions underlying the theory;
2 an explanation of the acquisition of helpful and unhelpful behaviour;
3 an explanation of the maintenance of helpful and unhelpful behaviour;
4 an explanation of how to help clients change their behaviour and consolidate their gains when counselling ends.

The first three of the above dimensions may be viewed as a theory's model of human development, whereas the final dimension is its model of practice. A theory's model of human development is relevant to whether people engage in either formal counselling or less formal helping contacts. A theory's model of practice is invariably stated by its originators in respect of formal counselling and psychotherapy and, in varying degrees, requires modifying for less formal helping.

Schools of counselling and helping

A useful distinction exists between *schools* of counselling and helping and *approaches* to counselling and helping. A theoretical approach presents a single position regarding the theory and practice of counselling and helping. A school of counselling and helping is a grouping of different theoretical approaches that are similar to one another in terms of certain important characteristics that distinguish them from theoretical approaches in other counselling and helping schools.

Probably the three main schools that influence contemporary counselling and psychotherapy practice are the psychodynamic school, the humanistic school and the cognitive-behavioural school. Sometimes the humanistic school incorporates existential therapeutic approaches and then gets the broader title of being the humanistic-existential school. Be careful not to exaggerate the differences between counselling and therapy schools, since there are similarities as well differences amongst them. Box 3.1 briefly describes some distinguishing features of the psychodynamic, humanistic and cognitive-behavioural schools.

Box 3.1   Three counselling and helping schools

The psychodynamic school

The term 'psychodynamic' refers to the transfer of *psychic or mental energy* between the different structures and levels of consciousness within people's minds. Psychodynamic approaches emphasize the importance of *unconscious influences* on how people function. Counselling aims to increase clients' abilities to exercise *greater conscious control* over their lives. *Analysis or interpretation of dreams* can be a central part of counselling.

The humanistic school

The humanistic school is based on humanism, a system of values and beliefs that emphasizes the better qualities of humankind and people's abilities to develop their *human potential*. Humanistic counsellors emphasize enhancing clients' abilities to *experience their feelings* and think and act in harmony with their underlying tendencies to *actualize themselves* as unique individuals.

The cognitive-behavioural school

Traditional behavioural counselling focuses mainly on changing *observable behaviours* by means of providing different or rewarding consequences. The cognitive-behavioural school broadens behavioural counselling to incorporate the contribution of *how people think* to creating, sustaining and changing their problems. In cognitive-behavioural approaches, counsellors *assess* clients and then *intervene* to help them to *change specific ways of thinking and behaving* that sustain their problems.

Approaches to counselling and helping

Box 3.2 presents what are probably the two main theoretical approaches from each of the three main counselling and helping schools. So that readers can obtain a sense of the history of the development of ideas within counselling and helping. I have included the dates of the originators of each approach. Those readers wishing to pursue their study of counselling and helping theory are referred to the annotated bibliography provided in Appendix 1 at the end of the book. The descriptions provided in Box 3.2 reflect the stance of the originators of the different positions, rather than developments within a theoretical approach stimulated by others.

Box 3.2 Six counselling and helping approaches

Psychodymanic school

Classical psychoanalysis *Originator: Sigmund Freud (1856–1939)*
Pays great attention to unconscious factors related to infantile sexuality in the development of neurosis. Psychoanalysis, which may last for many years, emphasizes working through the transference, in which clients perceive their therapists as reincarnations of important figures from their childhoods, and the interpretation of dreams.

Analytical therapy *Originator: Carl Jung (1875–1961)*
Divides the unconscious into the personal unconscious and the collective unconscious, the latter being a storehouse of universal archetypes and primordial images. Therapy includes analysis of the

transference, active imagination and dream analysis. Jung was particularly interested in working with clients in the second half of life.

Humanistic school

Person-centred therapy *Originator: Carl Rogers (1902–87)*
Lays great stress on the primacy of subjective experience and how clients can become out of touch with their actualising tendency through introjecting others' evaluations and treating them as if they were their own. Counselling emphasizes a relationship characterised by accurate empathy, respect and non-possessive warmth.

Gestalt therapy *Originator: Fritz Perls (1893–1970)*
Individuals become neurotic by losing touch with their senses and interfering with their capacity to make strong contact with their environments. Counselling emphasizes increasing clients' awareness and vitality through awareness techniques, experiments, sympathy and frustration, and dream work.

Cognitive-behavioural school

Rational emotive behaviour therapy *Originator: Albert Ellis (1913–)*
Emphasizes clients reindoctrinating themselves with irrational beliefs that lead to unwanted feelings and self-defeating actions. Counselling involves disputing clients irrational beliefs and replacing them with more rational beliefs. Elegant or profound counselling entails changing clients' philosophies of life.

Cognitive therapy *Originator: Aaron Beck (1921–)*
Clients become distressed because they are faulty processors of information with a tendency to jump to unwarranted conclusions. Therapy consists of educating clients in how to test the reality of their thinking by interventions such as Socratic questioning and conducting real-life experiments.

So far, I have presented the different schools and theoretical approaches as though they are separate. In reality, many counsellors regard themselves as working in either eclectic or integrative ways. A detailed discussion of eclecticism and integration is beyond the scope of this practical book. Suffice it for now to say that eclecticism is the practice of drawing from different counselling schools in formulating client problems and implementing treatment interventions. Integration refers to attempting to blend together theoretical concepts and/or practical interventions drawn from different counselling approaches into coherent and integrated wholes. To a large extent the counselling skills presented in this book are drawn from the humanistic and cognitive-behavioural schools and approaches.

Modes of counselling and helping

Another way of looking at counselling and helping is in terms of different modes or ways of using counselling skills with clients. Unlike counsellors and psychotherapists, helpers often use their counselling skills within each of these modes in informal rather than formal contexts. By far the most common mode is that of one-to-one or individual counselling and helping. Another mode is that of couples work, in which helpers work with partners or marital spouses. In some helping settings, such as schools and offices, couples work may be extended to working with problems between two teachers, students or workers. A further mode is that of family counselling and helping, in which families and their component parts are the target of using counselling skills. An example of helpers using counselling skills in a family mode would be that of school counsellors working with families to help unhappy pupils to perform better.

Still another mode for using counselling skills is that of group counselling and helping. In formal group counselling the optimum size for a group is often thought to be around six to eight members so as to allow for diversity, yet not become so large that individual members receive insufficient attention. Helpers may use counselling skills when working with groups of different sizes and with different agendas, for instance, supervisors in work groups or youth workers with groups of young people. Sometimes groups focus on the relationships between participants and on other occasions they can have more of a focus in the training of specific skills, for instance, health maintenance skills, job-seeking skills or study skills. In both kinds of groups, helpers can use counselling skills.

While the focus of this book is primarily on individual work, the basic counselling skills covered in it are relevant to other modes of working with clients. Modes of using counselling skills and theoretical approaches to counselling and helping interact in at least two important ways. First, most leading theoretical approaches to counselling and helping can be adapted from working in the individual mode to working in couples, family or group modes. For example, person-centred practitioners can work in individual, couples, family and group modes. Second, there may be special theoretical underpinnings that apply to the different modes. For example, there are many different theoretical approaches to family counselling and helping. Helpers who work in other modes beyond working with individuals must recognize that they will almost certainly require further counselling skills to be maximally effective in each additional mode.

Research and counselling and helping

Statements of counselling and helping approaches can be both based on research and stimulate research. For example, cognitive-behavioural therapy is based on research into how people think and into how both people and animals behave. Furthermore, cognitive-behavioural approaches, such as rational emotive behaviour therapy and cognitive therapy, have stimulated research into their processes and outcomes. There is a growing trend in counselling and psychotherapy to try and identify empirically supported treatments for different client problems. Overall, research evidence tends to support the cognitive-behavioural approaches, partly because they lend themselves to defining certain problems narrowly, unlike humanistic approaches which espouse more general personal growth goals. Needless to say, many clients' problems do not fit into neat packages.

Theories also provide counsellors and helpers with frameworks within which to make predictive hypotheses during their counselling and helping work. Whether acknowledging it or not, all helpers are practitioner-researchers. Helpers make hypotheses every time they decide how to work with specific clients and how to respond to a single or a series of client utterances.

Clients are also practitioner-researchers who make predictions about how best to lead their lives. If valid theories of counselling and helping are transmitted to clients, they may increase the accuracy with which clients can predict the consequences of their behaviours and, hence, gain more control over their lives.

Because of the mounting pressures to control the costs of providing counselling and helping services, a growing and interesting area of research is the extent to which helpers can provide competent services for particular problems more cheaply than accredited counsellors and psychotherapists. For example, nurses with thorough training and supervision in addressing specific healthcare problems may provide counselling help for these problems that compares favourably with that offered by accredited counsellors and psychotherapists. One reason for this is that nurses may possess years of prior experience in working with certain kinds of patients.

4   Helpers and clients as diverse persons

Helpers and clients bring numerous personal characteristics to their contacts with one another. For example, both helpers and clients have life histories of varying degrees of happiness and suffering. In addition, both helpers and clients have differing levels of poor and good mind skills and communication action/skills for coping with the problems and opportunities in their lives.

Over the past 20 to 30 years there has been a growing interest in diversity sensitive counselling and helping. Apart from their personal histories, all helpers and clients possess a mixture of different characteristics that they bring to their helping contacts. They also possess perceptions and evaluations of these different characteristics in themselves and others. There is no such thing as perfect helper–client matching, though there may be important and often desirable similarities, for example, regarding culture or race. Box 4.1 indicates just some of the many areas of diversity in the practice of counselling and helping. I briefly discuss each of these areas in turn.

Culture

In Britain, demographic data for the year 1999–2000 showed that 6.7 per cent or about 1 in 15 of the total population came from ethnic minorities. Australia and the US have proportionately much larger ethnic minority populations. Helpers and clients can come from different cultures and be at differing levels of assimilation to the mainstream culture. Even if they both come from the mainstream

---

Box 4.1 Ten areas of diversity in counselling and helping

1 **Culture** Ancestral origins in either the mainstream or in a minority group culture and, if the latter, one's degree of acculturation.

2 **Race** Possessing distinctive physical characteristics according to a racial sub-grouping or being of mixed race.

3 **Social class** Differences attached to such matters as income, educational attainment and occupational status.

4 **Biological sex** Female or male.

5 **Gender-role identity** Differences in feelings, thoughts and behaviour according to the social classification of attributes as 'feminine' or 'masculine'.

6 **Marital status** Single, cohabiting, married, separated, divorced, remarried or widowed.

7 **Sexual and affectionate orientation** Heterosexual, lesbian, gay or bisexual.

8 **Physical disability** A deficiency in the structure or functioning of some part of the body.

9 **Age** Childhood, adolescence, young adulthood, middle age, late middle age or old age.

10 **Religion or philosophy** Christian, Hindu, Muslim, Buddhist or some other religious or secular belief system.

---

culture they may have differing levels of adaptation or rejection of its main rules and conventions. Helpers and clients who are native-born of migrant parents may experience split loyalties between the pull of parental cultures and personal wishes to assimilate into mainstream culture.

Helpers and clients who are migrants may experience differing levels of repulsion and attraction both to their previous and new home cultures. Migrants always carry around part of their previous cultures in their hearts and heads. Some migrants are never really happy in their host countries. However, migrants idealizing previous cultures can get a rude awakening when they go home for the first time.

In addition to the cultures that helpers and clients bring, they each have differing experiences of how accepted they have been within their own and other cultures. Some will have been fortunate enough to have had their cultural differences accepted and cherished, while others will have received feedback that their cultures are inferior.

An important cultural issue relates to expectations about helper and client roles. For example, cultures may differ in their rules about whom they consider appropriate help givers, the appropriateness of disclosing personal information to strangers, how they exhibit different emotions and symptoms, and the degree of direction expected from helpers. In addition, cultures differ in their attitude to time and to the making and keeping of appointments.

Race

Helpers and clients may come from different races. Whereas cultural differences can be subtle, racial differences are readily observable. Both helpers and clients may have experienced or be experiencing racial discrimination in relation to the majority white host culture. Furthermore, sometimes those from majority cultures can feel suspicion and hostility when they venture into minority cultures. The idea of racially matching helpers and clients (black with black, Asian with Asian and so on) is not universally supported. However, many relationships between helpers and clients who are of different races involve working through and moving beyond racial stereotypes.

Social class

Social class is still a big issue in Britain and, to a lesser extent, in Australia and the US. Income, educational attainment and occupational status are currently three of the main measures of social class in Western countries. Other indicators include schooling, accent, clothing, manners, nature of social networks and type and location of housing.

Helpers and clients bring their social class into their relationships. They also bring their sensitivity to the effects of others' social class on them and their social class on others. If insufficiently skilled, social class considerations may create unnecessary barriers to establishing effective helping relationships. If helpers possess feelings of either inferiority or superiority on account of their social class, they should strive to eliminate them. Being an effective helper is difficult enough without the intrusion of avoidable social class agendas.

Biological sex

Helpers and clients bring their biological sex to their relationship. In most formal counselling settings, women outnumber men both as helpers and clients. This is less likely to be the case in settings were helpers are using counselling skills as part of other primary roles. In such instances, the sex ratio of helpers and clients may be more likely to reflect that of the working context, be it educational, health or business. Whether the helping relationship exists between people of the same sex or of different sexes it is likely to influence the quantity and quality of the communication within it, but this may be for better or worse depending on those involved.

Gender-role identity

Gender also refers to the social and cultural classification of attributes and behaviours as 'masculine' and 'feminine'. Helpers and clients bring their gender or sex-role identities to the relationship – how they view themselves and one another on the dimensions of 'masculinity' and 'femininity' and the importance they attach to these constructs.

Helpers and clients can be categorized according to the importance they attach to gender issues: for instance, to what extent and in what ways they are advocates for women's or men's issues. Furthermore, both parties may vary in the extent to which they possess sexist views that assume the superiority of one sex over the other.

Marital status

Though especially among younger people, there is a trend towards people cohabiting outside of marriage: nevertheless, by far the most adults in Western countries still get married. In most instances where helpers use counselling skills as parts of other primary roles, their marital status is likely to be considered irrelevant by themselves and by their clients. However, when helpers assist clients in improving their intimate relationships, their marital status could be an issue for some clients.

Sexual and affectionate orientation

Helpers and clients bring their sexual orientation to the helping relationship whether they are heterosexual, lesbian, gay or bisexual. I use the term 'sexual orientation' rather than sexual preference. Many, if not most, predominantly lesbian and gay people's sexual orientation is a fact of life, based on genetics and significant learning experiences, rather than a preference based on free choice. Sometimes the term 'affectionate orientation' is now used as a way of acknowledging that in same sex relationships, as in opposite sex ones, there are many other aspects than the sexual.

Helpers and clients not only bring their sexual and affectionate orientation to helping relationships, they bring their thoughts and feelings about their own and other people's sexual orientation too. Lesbian, gay and bisexual helpers and clients may be at varying levels of acceptance of their own and other people's homosexuality. In addition, lesbian and gay clients may wonder about the sexual orientation and attitudes of helpers. They may fear that their helpers will have difficulty accepting them.

Probably few helpers are openly homophobic, but many may, in varying degrees, be heterosexist. By heterosexist, I mean that either knowingly or unknowingly such helpers assume the superiority of demonstrating affection towards members of the opposite sex. On the other hand, some lesbian and gay helpers may have difficulty working with repressed heterosexuality or the openly heterosexual components of bisexual clients. Wittingly or unwittingly, they may seek to influence such clients into lesbian and gay moulds.

Age

Immediately helpers and clients meet for the first time they will start making assumptions about and connected with one another's age. Assessment of age is the starting point for other thoughts and feelings about themselves and one another. For example, young helpers may perceive themselves as being out of their depths with older clients since they do not have sufficient life experience. Young clients may fear that older helpers will be unable to understand them on account of the generation or generations gap.

Age is partly a physical concept, but it is also an attitude of mind. Older people can be psychologically alive and vibrant, whereas some young people are mentally rigid. Also, how helpers and clients communicate can reinforce or dispel assumptions based on physical age.

For example, youthful helpers can communicate in calm and comfortable ways that reassure older clients, while older helpers can show understanding of their young clients' culture and aspirations.

Physical disability

Either the helper or the client or both may be physically disabled in some way. Many people suffer from mobility, hearing, sight and other impairments. Sometimes these impairments are genetic and on other occasions are the result of life events, such as industrial or car accidents or military service. Helpers and clients will also have thoughts and feelings about their own and one another's disabilities. Some helpers may rightly feel inadequately skilled to work with certain physically disabled clients.

Being a physically disabled helper raises many issues. All physically disabled people have to come to terms with their physical restrictions. Many physically disabled helpers have become calmer and stronger people if they have successfully navigated the emotional ramifications of their disabilities. Charles Moreland, at the time of writing the Chairman of the Leonard Cheshire Foundation, is an inspiring example of someone who has grown through suffering. For the past 20 years he has had multiple sclerosis, which is a chronic and, in his case, progressive disease of the central nervous system which has left him unable to walk. Eleven years ago he retired from his career as a banker and became a volunteer with the foundation. Moreland now uses basic counselling skills as part of his high-profile primary role.

Sometimes helpers may be under pressure to change the nature of the helping relationship because of other agendas connected with disabled clients: for example, pressure from insurers or workers' compensation boards for brief helping or to write reports about clients. Though very much a minority, some disabled clients may allow financial claim considerations to sabotage the integrity of their helping relationships.

Religion or philosophy

Helpers and clients bring their religious beliefs, spiritual yearnings and explanations of the meaning of life to their relationships. Such beliefs can be sources of strength. For example, in Western cultures many helpers are strongly motivated by the Christian concept of *agape* or unselfish love. Furthermore, sharing the same religious beliefs as clients can strengthen a collaborative working relationship.

Helpers differ in their abilities to develop relationships with clients whose attitudes towards religion and spirituality differ from their own. An issue for many religious helpers is the extent to which the values and teachings of their church influence how they work. For instance, Roman Catholic helpers may face value conflicts with clients in areas such as divorce, contraception, abortion and pre-marital or lesbian and gay sex.

In the above I have reviewed ten key characteristics that helpers and clients bring to their helping contacts and relationships. Helper and client personal characteristics come in different permutations and combinations. No helping relationship exists in a vacuum. Helpers require sensitivity to the effect that their own and their clients' personal characteristics have on how they communicate and on how they can best develop their helping relationship. Helpers also need to be realistic about their limitations and be prepared to refer clients to other helpers who might understand their special circumstances better.

5   The helping relationship

In Chapter 1 I mentioned that helping relationships are often not as formal and clearly structured as counselling and psychotherapy relationships. A reason for this is that many helpers are using counselling skills in the context of other relationships, for instance, social worker–client or supervisor–worker. The idea of weekly 45 to 50 minute counselling sessions conducted in offices set aside for this purpose scarcely applies to large numbers of contacts between helpers and clients. Sometimes helpers employ counselling skills in fairly long sessions, say when offering support after bereavements or when conducting employment appraisals. Often, however, helpers use counselling skills in contacts with clients that are relatively brief, say 10 to 15 minutes, and intermittent, as need arises. Furthermore, though some helping relationships take place in counselling rooms, many helpers use their counselling skills in offices, hospital wards, classrooms, tutorial rooms, living rooms and factory canteen settings, among other locations. Consequently, readers need to adapt the following discussion of helping relationships to the contexts in which they either use or will be using counselling skills.

Dimensions of helping relationships

Connection is the essential characteristic of any relationship. Helping relationships are the human connections between helpers and clients both in their direct dealings and in one another's heads. Within the overall relationship between helper and client, there are a number of dimensions or strands.

The public or observable relationship consists of all the communications relevant to any particular helper–client relationship. During helping contacts, both helper and client send and receive numerous verbal, vocal and body messages. In addition, helpers may provide clients with written material, use a whiteboard, and sometimes make cassettes and/or videotapes. After helping, there may be further face-to-face contact or contact by phone, letter or email.

Helping relationships take place in both participants' minds as well as in external communication. Many helpers and clients have working relationships that precede or accompany their helping relationships and, consequently, have already started forming impressions of one another. During face-to-face helping both participants relate to one another in their minds, for example, clients may be deciding how far to trust helpers, how much to reveal, when and in what ways. In addition, both participants are constantly forming and reforming mental conceptions of one another. Furthermore, in the periods between their helping sessions and contacts, helpers and clients engage in a mental relationship when thinking or fantasizing about one another and when reviewing material they have discussed together.

Core conditions of helping relationships

In 1957, Carl Rogers published a seminal article entitled 'The necessary and sufficient conditions of therapeutic personality change'. In this article, Rogers identified six conditions for therapeutic change, three of which – empathic understanding, unconditional positive regard and congruence – are often referred to as the core conditions of helping relationships. In this book, I do not use the terms empathic understanding, unconditional positive regard and congruence, but use different terms to break down the counselling skills covered by these concepts. However, here I briefly describe each of the core conditions for two main reasons. First, the concepts provide valuable insights into how to strengthen rather than interfere with developing collaborative working relationships with clients. Second, the terms empathy, unconditional regard and congruence are in such common use in the helping professions that readers should know what they mean.

Empathy

Clients like to feel understood on their own terms by helpers. Empathy is the capacity to identify oneself mentally with and fully to comprehend the client's inner world. Helpers may possess and be perceived to show empathic understanding in relation to single client statements, a series of client statements, the whole of a helping session, or a series of helping sessions. Rogers thought helpers should possess and show an empathic attitude. He stressed creating an empathic emotional climate in the helping interview rather than using empathy as a set of skills.

Rogers' use of the term 'empathy' particularly focused on the construct of experiencing. He attempted to improve the quantity and quality of his clients' inner listening to the ongoing flow of psychological and physiological experiencing within them. As well as helping clients to get in touch with more obvious feelings, he attempted to help them sense meanings of which they were scarcely aware. However, he stopped short of trying to uncover those emotions of which clients were totally unaware, since this would be too threatening.

Empathy is an active process in which helpers desire to know and reach out to receive clients' communications and meanings. Responding to individual client statements is a process of listening and observing, resonating, discriminating, communicating and checking one's understanding. Needless to say, the final and essential dimension is that the client has, to some extent, perceived the helper's empathy. Box 5.1, taken from a demonstration film with Rogers as the counsellor, illustrates this process. The client, Gloria, is talking about how her father could never show he cared for her the way she would have liked.

Box 5.1 Dimensions of the empathy process

Client's statement:	'I don't know what it is. You know when I talk about it, it feels more flip. If I just sit still a minute, it feels like a great big hurt down there. Instead, I feel cheated.'

Counsellor's responding processes

Observing and listening:	Observes and listens to the client's verbal, vocal and bodily communication.
Resonating:	Feels some of the emotion the client experiences.
Discriminating:	Discriminates what is really important to the client and formulates this into a response.

Communicating:	'Its much easier to be a little flip because then you don't feel that big lump inside of hurt.' Communicates a response that attempts to show understanding of the client's thoughts, feelings and personal meanings. Accompanies verbal with good vocal and bodily communication.
Checking:	In this instance, the client quickly made her next statement that followed the train of her experiencing and thought. However, the counsellor could either have waited and allowed the client space to respond or could have inquired if the response was accurate.

Client perception of counsellor's responding

How the client reacted indicated she perceived that the counsellor showed excellent empathy and that she was able to continue getting more in touch with her experiencing.

Unconditional positive regard

Unconditional positive regard consists of two dimensions: level of regard and unconditionality of regard. Level of regard, or possibly more correctly level of positive regard, consists of positive helper feelings towards the client like liking, caring and warmth. Unconditionality of regard consists of a non-judgmental acceptance of the client's experiencing and disclosures as their subjective reality. A key issue in unconditional positive regard is that helpers are not trying to possess or control clients to meet their own needs. Instead, helpers respect clients' separateness and accept their unique differences. Such acceptance gives clients permission to acknowledge and fully experience their thoughts and feelings.

Another way of looking at unconditional positive regard is that helpers respect and value the deeper core of clients and identify with their potential rather than with their current behaviours. Unconditional positive regard involves compassion for human frailty and an understanding of universal conditions which lead individuals to become less effective persons than desirable. Clients are more likely to blossom and change if prized for their human potential rather than rejected for their human failings. Though I realize that this may be setting very high standards, I consider that often the inability of helpers to feel and show unconditional positive regard reflects their own insufficient personal development.

Congruence

Congruence or genuineness has both an internal and an external dimension. Internally, helpers are able to accurately acknowledge their significant thoughts, feelings and experiences. They possess a high degree of self-awareness. This self-awareness may include acknowledging parts of themselves that are not ideal for helping: for example, 'I am afraid of this client' or 'My attention is so focused on my own problems that I am scarcely able to listen to him/her.'

Externally, helpers communicate to clients as real persons. What helpers say and how they say it rings true. They do not hide behind professional facades or wear polite social masks. Honesty and sincerity characterize congruent communication. For example, compassionate and caring helpers live these qualities in their helping encounters. Their verbal, vocal and bodily communication sends consistent caring messages. They are not portraying how they think they should be but communicating how they truly are in those moments.

Congruence does not mean 'letting it all hang out'. Helpers are able to use their awareness of their own thoughts and feelings to nurture and develop their clients. Though congruence may include personal disclosures, these disclosures are for the benefit of clients in the interest of humanizing the helping process and moving it forward and not in order to make helpers feel more comfortable.

Communication processes and patterns

Helping relationships are processes of two-way communication for good or ill. For example, during helping sessions and contacts, helpers and clients are in a continuous process of sending, receiving, evaluating and interpreting verbal, vocal and bodily communication.

One way to look at the communication processes involved in helping relationships is in terms of how helpers and clients reward one another. For example, helper communications like active listening, warmth, and invitations for clients to become involved in the process can each be rewarding to clients. Clients also provide rewards to their helpers, for instance, smiles and head nods.

As in any relationship, helpers and clients can build up mutually reinforcing communication patterns, which can enhance or impede the helping process. A helpful pattern of communication is one that is collaborative in attaining legitimate helping goals. For example, good empathic responses from helpers elicit honest self-exploring responses from clients, which in turn elicit good empathic responses from helpers and so on.

The demand–withdrawal pattern is an example of an unhelpful pattern of communication. Here helpers continually seek personal data from clients who constantly withdraw in face of such attempts because they are not ready to reveal the required information. On the other hand, sometimes under-confident helpers are too reticent in seeking information. Another negative communication pattern is that between charismatic or domineering helpers and dependent clients. A further unhelpful communication pattern occurs between talkative helpers and quiet clients. A related negative communication pattern is that of helpers who take control by constantly asking questions and then find themselves with clients who are waiting for the next question rather than voluntarily offering information about themselves.

The collaborative working relationship

A good way to look at successful helping relationships, especially those that extend over a period of time, is to consider whether they are collaborative working relationships. This is a valuable criterion to whether helpers are using counselling skills in quasi-counselling roles, as part of other primary roles, as voluntary helpers or are providing one another with peer support. The notion of collaboration implies that clients cooperate with helpers because they feel understood by them and, within the limitations of the contexts in which they encounter one another, feel some kind of positive emotional bond with them. Collaborative working relationships also assume that helpers and clients are working towards mutual goals. Furthermore, collaboration entails clients being comfortable with the tasks and methods employed in helping.

6   The helping process

Helpers see clients in a wide variety of contexts and with many different primary and secondary agendas. Furthermore, their contact with clients may be brief and intermittent rather than on a regular basis. To assume that there is a single helping process that covers all these situations is inaccurate. Nevertheless, many helpers, helper trainers and helping students find it useful to think of their use of counselling skills with clients as constituting a helping process.

When thinking of counselling and helping, the word 'process' has at least two main meanings. One meaning is that of movement, the fact of something happening. Such processes can take place within helpers and clients and between them. Furthermore, helping processes can take place outside as well as inside helping relationships and after as well as during helping relationships. Another meaning of the word 'process' is that of progression over time, especially a progression which involves a series of stages. The two meanings of the word 'process' overlap, in that the processes within and between helpers and clients change as helping progresses through various stages.

Helping process models are simplified step-by-step representations of different goals and activities at progressive stages of helping. They are structured frameworks for viewing the helping process. They provide ways of assisting counselling skills students and helpers to think and work more systematically. Helping process models work on the assumption that the use of helping skills is cumulative, and that insufficient application of skills in the earlier stage or stages negatively influences the ability to help in later stages.

In this chapter I present a simple three-stage model of the helping process. The underlying idea is that many clients come to see helpers with fairly specific problems. Sometimes, the problems may have a large psychological component, like learning to set limits assertively on unwanted sexual advances. On other occasions, clients may bring problems to helpers that, on the surface at least, do not contain complex psychological components, such as needing financial, legal or retirement planning advice.

When applying helping models, a useful distinction to bear in mind is that between an overall problem (coping with sexual harassment) and specific situations within an overall problem (addressing a specific episode of sexual harassment, for example, dealing with a work colleague who will not take 'no' for an answer). My experience in training numerous students to use counselling skills is that it is best to start learning how to apply a helping process by working with specific situations within overall problems rather than with overall problems in their totality. However, in some kinds of helping, for instance financial or careers advice, an approach to training based on such a distinction may not be valid.

With helping models a further issue is that of how much to focus on identifying and changing clients' poor mind skills and communication/action skills that may not only contribute to their current problems but place them at risk of repeating their mistakes in future. In brief or intermittent helping, helpers may consider that there is neither sufficient opportunity nor enough client motivation for addressing such underlying issues, but this need not always be the case.

The Relating–Understanding–Changing (RUC) helping model

In this book I present a simple Relating–Understanding–Changing (RUC) helping process model (see Box 6.1) This model is especially applicable to problem situations, but can be adapted to where helpers have other agendas, for instance pregnancy advice, as well. The fact that the helping model is presented in three stages may imply a degree of tidiness inappropriate to the actual practice of helping. Often the stages overlap and sometimes helpers find it necessary to move backwards and forwards between stages. Flexibility can be important.

> **Box 6.1 The Relating–Understanding–Changing (RUC) helping model**
>
> **Stage 1: Relating**
> *Main task:* To start establishing a collaborative working relationship.
>
> **Stage 2: Understanding**
> *Main task:* To clarify and enlarge both helper and client understanding of the problem situation.
>
> **Stage 3: Changing**
> *Main task:* To assist the client to change so that the problem situation is addressed more effectively than in the past.

Stage 1 Relating

Here the main helper and client task is to start establishing a collaborative working relationship. Helping relationships start at, if not before, the point at which helpers first meet with clients. For instance, how helpers handle a telephone call may decide whether a client wishes to set up an appointment with them. Also helpers need to calm themselves down and get their helping space ready before they open the door of their offices to meet clients. A preliminary phase of the relating stage is the introductions phase, the purpose of which can be described as meeting, greeting and seating.

How helpers start a session varies according to the helping context as well as according to each participant's wishes. For example, helping contexts can require basic information gathering at the start of sessions. Apart from this, the main choice in starting a session is whether first to allow clients to tell their stories and then do some structuring about the nature of the helping contact or the reverse. My preference is for letting clients talk first and 'get their problem(s) off their chest'. Sometimes, clients come with one clearly identified problem situation, for example, how to handle anxiety concerning an important exam in a week's time. On other occasions, they may have many or more complex problems. In any event, helpers should use active listening skills to create an emotionally safe space for clients to share their main reasons for coming for help. If there is more than one problem area, helpers can summarize and identify the different problem areas and ask clients which one they want to address. Then, assuming the helping contact is brief, helpers can ask them to identify a particular situation within the problem area on which to work together.

Stage 2 Understanding

Here the main helper and client task is to clarify and enlarge their understanding of the chosen problem situation. Often clients feel at an impasse in problem situations. Getting them to describe the situation more fully in a supportive emotional climate can loosen their thinking, enlighten them and encourage them to think that they may be able to manage it better. In the context of good active listening skills, helpers can use questioning skills that elicit information about clients in relation to their problem situations. Areas in which helpers may ask questions include clients' thoughts, feelings and physical reactions and how they have attempted to cope in the past, including the patterns of communication they have established with significant others. Sometimes helpers engage clients in mini role-plays that can go some way to eliciting the actual verbal, vocal and bodily communications that they have employed in the problem situations.

Helpers seek to enlarge as well as to clarify the clients' understanding of such situations, including their contribution to sustaining negative aspects of them. Helpers may ask questions that elicit information relevant to the clients' mental processes, for instance about their self-talk, rules and perceptions. Sometimes helpers may challenge client perceptions and provide feedback. Furthermore, at appropriate junctures, helpers may summarize the ground recently covered. In addition, at the end of the understanding stage, helpers can summarize all the main points elicited so far and check with clients about the accuracy of their summary and whether they wish to modify, add or subtract anything.

Stage 3 Changing

Here the main helper and client task is for clients to change so that they deal with problem situations more effectively than in the past. Helpers and clients set goals and develop and implement strategies to address problem situations and to communicate, act and think better. Furthermore, they attend to how clients can maintain helpful changes.

Two somewhat overlapping approaches that helpers and clients can take to the changing stage are the facilitating problem-solving approach and the improving communications/actions and thoughts approach. In the facilitating problem-solving approach, helpers assist clients to clarify goals for problem situations, generate and explore options to attain them, and develop and implement action plans.

In the improving communications/actions and thoughts approach, helpers and clients work together to specify communication and thoughts goals and the strategies to attain each of them. They may explore options in regard to which goals to set. Often statements of goals can include not only what clients want to achieve but the communication they want to avoid as well. Helpers can assist clients to develop plans to attain their communication and thoughts goals. Frequently, helpers act as client-centred coaches in assisting clients to develop more effective verbal, vocal and body messages for their problem situations. Helpers should avoid controlling clients, assuming responsibility for their problems and making their decisions for them. Instead, helpers should encourage client autonomy by keeping clients 'owning' their problems. Skilled helpers draw out clients' own ideas and give them confidence in their own resources for handling their problem situations.

Sometimes coaching includes role-playing. Some helpers incorporate the use of the whiteboard into their coaching: for instance, jointly formulating with a client a clear verbal request for someone to change their behaviour and then pinpointing desirable vocal and body messages to back up this request. In addition, helpers can encourage clients to think more effectively. For instance, once clients have identified useful ways of communicating in their problem situations, helpers can coach them in helpful self-talk for rehearsing and enacting this behaviour in real life. Furthermore, helpers can assist clients to challenge unrealistic rules and perceptions and replace them with more realistic ones.

Helpers can encourage clients to rehearse and practice their new ways of thinking and communicating between sessions and then report back at the start of subsequent sessions. They encourage clients to assume responsibility for changing their behaviour both now and in future. Before helping ends, helpers and clients review ways that clients can maintain beneficial changes afterwards. Box 6.2 shows three examples of the RUC helping process model in action.

Box 6.2 Case examples

Example 1 Doing telephone counselling with a client about HIV/AIDS

Ron, 27, a telephone counsellor for an HIV/AIDS counselling service, receives a call from Danny, 22, who is worried that he may have contracted HIV. Ron builds a relationship with Danny by sensitively allowing him to share his fears. Ron then seeks to clarify and enlarge both his and Danny's understanding by gently probing how Danny has actually behaved and the extent to which he is likely to engage in high-risk behaviours in future. Though, on the basis of Danny's answers, Ron thinks it unlikely that he is HIV positive, together they review Danny's options for future action. These options include going to a recommended physician for HIV testing, getting sound information on how to prevent HIV/AIDS and on how to live with being HIV positive, and where Danny can go if he wants future counselling about his worries. The telephone conversation lasted about 25 minutes.

Example 2 Helping a couple to plan financially for their retirement

Debbie, 37, works in the asset management section of a large bank where she uses her counselling skills to assist Jennie and Frank, both in their mid-50s, to plan for their retirement. Debbie builds a relationship with Jennie and Frank by greeting them warmly and using good active listening skills as they describe their current situation and worries about the future. Interspersing questions with active listening, Debbie then clarifies some of Jennie and Frank's answers to a financial planning questionnaire they had completed earlier. Debbie also uses counselling skills to help Jennie and Frank articulate their goals for the future and the level of risk with which they are comfortable. At a subsequent session, Debbie presents a financial plan to Jennie and Frank and then further uses her counselling skills to help the couple give honest reactions to her proposals, which she then amends slightly in light of their feedback.

Example 3 Helping a worker with public speaking anxiety

When Kylie, 33, a pharmaceuticals sales representative, is asked by her sales manager to make a presentation at her company's annual sales conference in three week's time she is absolutely terrified. She goes to Tony, 44, her supervisor, who allows her to share her fears about making a fool of herself in public. Tony, who used to have a similar problem, asks Kylie about her previous experiences of public speaking and tries to identify what she is saying to herself that makes her so afraid now. Together Kylie and Tony identify come calming self-statements that Kylie can tell herself. Tony also agrees to spend some time coaching Kylie in how to prepare and deliver her forthcoming talk.

PART II

Specific counselling skills

7   Understanding the internal frame of reference

How many people do you know who listen to you properly? Most of us know very few. Quite apart from wanting air time to speak about their own thoughts, feelings and experiences, many people we know will put their own 'spin' on what we say rather than listen accurately and deeply to us. The single most important goal of any basic counselling and helping skills course is to improve the quality of students' listening. Even experienced counsellors and helpers have to monitor the quality of their listening all the time

Use active listening

Two counsellors meet in a lift at the end of a working day. One is looking fresh, the other tired.

Tired looking counsellor: 'I don't know how you can look so fresh after all that listening.'

Fresh looking counsellor: 'Who listens?'

How can helpers create an emotional climate so that their clients feel safe and free to talk with them? Many of the component skills of creating collaborative working relationships come under the heading of active listening. A distinction exists between hearing and listening. *Hearing* involves the capacity to be aware of and to receive sounds. *Listening* involves not only receiving sounds but, as much as possible, accurately understanding their meaning. As such it entails hearing and memorizing words, being sensitive to vocal cues, observing body language, and taking into account the personal and social context of communications. However, helpers can listen accurately without being a rewarding listener. *Active listening* entails helpers in not only accurately understanding speakers' communications, but also showing that they have understood. As such, active listening involves skills in both receiving and sending communications.

Active listening is the fundamental skill of any helping relationship. Nevertheless, throughout the Relating–Understanding–Changing helping model, helpers should adapt how they use active listening in the different stages of the model. Furthermore, if the model is unsuitable for the kind of helping contacts they have, helpers can adapt their skills of active listening accordingly. However, if helpers are unable to listen properly in the first place, they are poorly equipped to integrate active listening with other counselling skills, such as the ability to ask questions in an appropriate manner.

Possess an attitude of respect and acceptance

Four kinds of listening take place in any person-to-person helping conversation. Helper and client listen to messages from one another and also each listens to what is going on inside herself or himself. The quality of a helper's inner listening, or being appropriately sensitive to her or his own thoughts and feelings, may be vital to the quality of their outer listening. If either the helper or the client listen either poorly or excessively to themselves, they listen less well to one another. Conversely, if either or both listen well to one another, this may help the quality of their inner listening.

An accepting attitude involves respecting clients as separate human beings with rights to their own thoughts and feelings. Such an attitude entails suspending judgement on clients' perceived goodness or badness. All humans are fallible and possess good and poor human being skills or capabilities that may result in either happiness or suffering for themselves and others. Respect comes from the Latin word *respicere*, meaning to look at. Respect means the ability to look at others as they are and to prize their unique individuality. Respect also means allowing other people to grow and develop on their own terms without exploitation and control. Though an accepting attitude involves respecting others as separate and unique human beings, this does not mean that helpers need to agree with everything their clients say. Ideally, however, helpers are secure enough in themselves to respect what clients say as being their versions of reality.

Helpers need to be psychologically present to clients. This entails absence of defensiveness and a willingness to allow clients' expressions and experiencing to affect them. As much as possible, helpers should be 'all there' – with their body, thoughts, senses and emotions. Psychological accessibility entails an accepting attitude, not only to clients but also to oneself. Put simply, a confident person's acceptance of self translates into acceptance of others, whereas the reverse is also true.

Understand the client's internal frame of reference

Taking the client's perspective is another way of stating the ability to understand the internal frame of reference. There is an American Indian proverb that states: 'Don't judge any person until you have walked two moons in their moccasins.' If clients are to feel that helpers receive them loud and clear, they need to develop the ability to 'walk in their moccasins', 'get inside their skins' and 'see the world through their eyes'. At the heart of active listening is a basic distinction between 'you' and 'me', between 'your view of you' and 'my view of you', and between 'your view of me' and 'my view of me'. Your view of you and my view of me are inside or internal perspectives, whereas your view of me and my view of you are outside or external perspectives.

The skill of listening to and understanding clients is based on choosing to acknowledge the separateness between 'me' and 'you' by getting inside their internal frame of reference rather than remaining in one's own external frame of reference. If helpers respond to what clients say in ways that show accurate understanding of their perspectives, they respond as if inside the client's internal frame of reference. However, if helpers choose not to show understanding of their clients' perspectives or lack the skills to understand them, they respond from the external frame of reference. Box 7.1 provides examples of helper responses from external and internal frames of reference.

Often helpers can show that they are taking their client's internal frame of reference by starting their response with 'You'. However, as the statement 'You should show you care more' indicates, helpers can make responses starting with the word 'You' from the external frame of reference too.

Helpers should always consciously choose whether or not to respond as if inside their clients' internal frame of reference. Think of a three-link chain: client statement – helper response – client statement.

> **Box 7.1 Helper responses from internal and external frames of reference**
>
> **External frame of reference responses**
> 'Well, there were other ways you could have handled your in-laws.'
>
> 'Let me tell you about a similar experience I had to yours.'
>
> 'All men/women are bastards.'
>
> 'You should show you care more.'
>
> 'You're a very gentle sort of person.'
>
> **Internal frame of reference responses**
> 'You're frightened at the news that you have prostate cancer.'
>
> 'You have mixed feelings about turning down the marriage proposal.'
>
> 'You're delighted with your new parish priest.'
>
> 'You really appreciate how understanding your lawyer was about your accident.'
>
> 'You're feeling insecure about your job in the upcoming takeover.'

Helpers who respond from clients' internal frames of reference allow them to choose either to continue on the same path or to change direction. However, if helpers respond from their external frames of reference, they can influence clients in such a way as to divert or block those trains of thoughts, feelings and experiences that they might otherwise have chosen.

Introduction to activities

Each chapter in Part II of this book ends with an activity or activities to help readers to develop their knowledge and skills. Though my assumption is that readers are learning basic counselling skills in training groups, this may not always be the case. Nevertheless, readers may still want to perform some or all of the activities either with a partner or, if this is inconvenient, on one's own. Readers will enhance the value of this book if they undertake the activities diligently. While practice may not make perfect, it certainly can increase competence.

Trainers and students can decide how to proceed with each activity: for instance, whether the activity should be done as a whole group exercise, in threes, pairs, individually or using any combination of these approaches. When doing the activities, all concerned should ensure that no one feels under pressure to reveal any personal information that she or he does not want to. To save repetition, I only mention these instructions once here and not at the start of each activity.

ACTIVITIES

Activity 7.1 Identifying the client's internal frame of reference

Below are some statement-response excerpts from formal and informal helping situations. Three helper responses have been provided for each statement. Write 'IN' or 'EX' by each response according to whether it reflects the client's internal perspective or comes from the helper's external perspective. Some of the responses may seem artificial, but they have been chosen to highlight the point of the exercise. Answers are provided at the end of this chapter.

Example
Client to youth worker
Client: Some of my mates are on speed. I've tried it, but am worried that I might get hooked on a habit I can't afford.
Youth worker:

EX   (a) I wouldn't take drugs it if I were you.
EX   (b) How did you like it when you tried speed?
IN   (c) You're scared about starting an expensive habit that you might not be able to quit.

1 Unemployed worker to employment counsellor
Unemployed worker: I've got this big interview coming up and I'm afraid of messing it up.
Employment counsellor:

_____ (a) This is a case of performance anxiety.
_____ (b) You're worried about making a hash of this important event.
_____ (c) You should prepare thoroughly.

2 Patient to physiotherapist

Patient: I'll never get used to having my right leg amputated just above my knee.
Physiotherapist:

_____ (a) Well, wait and see how much progress we make together.
_____ (b) The doctor says that you are doing just fine.
_____ (c) You're pessimistic about adjusting to your loss.

3 Primary school student to teacher

Student: I'm unhappy because nobody likes me here. I want to go home.
Teacher:

_____ (a) You're upset and lonely here.
_____ (b) Many children take time to adjust to a new school.
_____ (c) School does not end for another hour.

Activity 7.2 Observing and assessing internal and external responses

1 Watch and listen to television and radio interviews and chat shows. Observe the extent to which interviewers respond from the interviewee's internal frame of reference.
2 Monitor your own communication for a week and become more aware of when you respond to speakers from your own or from their frame of reference.
   (a) in helping contacts, and
   (b) in daily life.

Answers to Activity 7.1

1	(a) EX	(b) IN	(c) EX
2	(a) EX	(b) EX	(c) IN
3	(a) IN	(b) EX	(c) EX

8   Showing attention and interest

When together, helpers and clients always send messages to one another. In Chapter 2, I mentioned that there were five main ways of sending communication/action skills messages, namely: verbal, vocal, bodily, touch and action-taking messages. This chapter aims to build readers' skills in sending good body messages to clients. Helpers' body messages as listeners are important both when listening to and responding to clients. To be a rewarding person with whom to talk, helpers need physically to convey their emotional availability and interest. Often this is referred to as 'attending behaviour'.

Body messages are the main category of helper responses when clients are speaking. A simple example of what not to do may highlight the point. Imagine being a client who comes to a helper for assistance with a sensitive personal problem and, when the helper asks you to say why you have come, she or he looks out of the window and puts their feet up on the desk. On a more serious note, as a counselling graduate student at Stanford University in California, I had an excellent client-centred counsellor who was the Director of what was then called the Counseling and Testing Center. Every now and then he would put his feet up on his desk in a relaxed manner. However, by then I knew he was still attending closely to me and I did not find his behaviour at all off-putting.

The following suggestions include some of the main body message skills that demonstrate interest and attention. In varying degrees, they provide non-verbal rewards for talking. I offer this list of suggestions with the proviso that helpers who see clients in non-office settings will have to edit or adapt the suggestions to their different helping contexts.

Be available

It may seem obvious, but helpers may sometimes rightly or wrongly be perceived as insufficiently available to help. They may be overworked. They may be poor at letting their availability or any limits on it be known. Intentionally or unintentionally, they may send messages that create distance. For instance, a minority of college and university lecturers may rarely be around during their office hours for discussing students' concerns. In addition, they may spend as little time on campus as they can get away with. Helpers need to send clear messages to clients and others about availability and access. One simple way to indicate availability in informal helping settings is just to go over and be near or chat to people.

Adopt a relaxed and open body posture

A relaxed body posture, without slumping or slouching, contributes to the message that a helper is receptive. If helpers sit in a tense and uptight fashion, their clients may consciously or intuitively feel that they are too bound up in their personal agendas and unfinished business to be fully accessible.

Helpers and clients need to sit with an open body posture so that they can easily see one another. Some counselling skills trainers recommend sitting square to clients – the helper's left shoulder opposite the client's right shoulder. However, another option is to sit at a slight angle to clients. Here, both people can still receive all of one another's significant facial and bodily messages. The advantage of this is that it provides each person with more discretion in varying the directness of their contact than if sitting opposite one another. Highly vulnerable clients may especially appreciate this seating arrangement.

How helpers use their arms and legs can enhance or detract from an open body posture. For example, crossed arms can be perceived as barriers – sometimes, crossed legs can too. There is some research evidence that suggests that postural similarity, where two people take up mirror-image postures, is perceived as a sign of liking.

Lean slightly forward

Whether helpers lean forwards, backwards or sideways is another aspect of their body posture. If they lean too far forward they look odd and clients may experience an invasion of their personal space.

However, in moments of intimate disclosure, a marked forward lean may build rapport rather than be perceived as intrusive. If helpers lean too far back, clients may find this posture to be distancing. Especially at the start of helping, a slight forward trunk lean can encourage clients, without threatening them.

Use appropriate gaze and eye contact

Gaze means looking at people in the area of their faces. Good gaze skills indicate a helper's interest and enable them to receive important facial messages. Gaze can give helpers cues about when to stop listening and start responding. However, the main cues used in synchronizing conversation are verbal and voice messages rather than body messages.

Good eye-contact skills involve helpers looking in the client's direction in order to allow the possibility of their eyes meeting reasonably often. There is an equilibrium level for eye contact in any helping relationship, depending on the degree of anxiety in client and helper, how developed the relationship is, and the degree of attraction involved. Staring can threaten clients because they may feel dominated or seen through. I once had a client who started counselling by sitting with one hand shielding his eyes, looking 90 degrees from me, and only occasionally taking a quick peek in my direction. It took about eight sessions for him gradually to move towards a normal amount of eye contact. Clients want an appropriate amount of eye contact from helpers and may perceive them as tense or bored if they look down or away too often.

Convey appropriate facial expressions

When discussing feelings in Chapter 2, I mentioned the seven important feelings – happiness, interest, surprise, fear, sadness, anger and disgust or contempt – each of which can be conveyed by facial expressions. People's faces are their main way of sending body messages about feelings. Much facial information is conveyed through the mouth and eyebrows. A friendly, relaxed facial expression, including a smile, usually demonstrates interest. However as the client talks, helpers' facial expressions need to show that they are tuned into what they say. For instance, if clients' are serious, weeping or angry, helpers need to adjust their facial expression to indicate that they understand their feelings.

Use good gestures

Gestures are body movements used to convey thoughts and feelings. Perhaps the head nod is the most common gesture in listening, with small ones to show continued attention, larger and repeated ones to indicate agreement. Head nods can be viewed as rewards to clients to continue talking. On the negative side, selective head nods can also be powerful ways of controlling clients. Then unconditional acceptance becomes conditional acceptance.

Gestures may also illustrate shapes, sizes or movements, particularly when these are difficult to describe in words. Helpers can respond with arm and hand gestures to show their attention and interest to clients. However, helpers using expressive arm gestures too much or too little can be off-putting. Negative gestures that can display inattentiveness and discourage clients from clear communication include fidgeting with pens and pencils, hands clenched together, finger drumming, fiddling with one's hair, one's hand over one's mouth, ear tugging and scratching oneself, among others.

Use touch sparingly

Touching clients may be appropriate in helping, though great care needs to be taken that it is not an unwanted invasion of personal space. For example, helper demonstrations of concern may include touching a client's hands, arms, shoulders and upper back. The intensity and duration of touch should be sufficient to establish contact, yet avoid discomfort and any hint of sexual interest. Part of being an active listener includes picking up messages about the limits and desirability of your use of touch. As porcupine parents advise their offspring about making love, when contemplating touching clients 'proceed with caution'.

Be sensitive to personal space and height

Active listening entails respecting clients' personal space. Helpers can be too close or too far away. Perhaps a comfortable physical distance for helpers and clients is sitting with their heads about five feet apart. In Western cultures clients might perceive any shorter distance as too personal. If helpers are physically too far away, not only do clients have to talk louder, but they may perceive them as emotionally distant. The most comfortable height for helping conversations is with both people's heads at the same level. Those helpers who sit in higher and more elaborate chairs than their clients can contribute to the latter persons' feeling less powerful in the relationship.

Be careful about clothing and grooming

Sometimes helpers' clothes are governed by the contexts in which they work, for instance, doctors wear white coats and nurses wear uniforms in hospitals. On many other occasions helpers can choose how they dress. Helpers' clothes send messages about themselves that can influence how much and in which areas clients reveal themselves. These messages include their social and occupational standing, sex-role identity, ethnicity, their degree of conformity to peer group norms, rebelliousness and how outgoing or introverted they are. While maintaining their individuality, helpers need to dress appropriately for their clientele, for example, delinquent teenagers respond better to informally dressed counsellors than do stressed business executives. Helpers' personal grooming also provides important information about how well they take care of themselves; for instance, they may be clean or dirty, neat or untidy. In addition, the length and styling of helpers' hair sends messages to clients about them.

Concluding comments

The concept of rules is very important for understanding the appropriateness of body messages. However, rules governing behaviour in helping situations should not be straightjackets and, sometimes, helpers may need to bend or break the rules to create genuinely collaborative helping relationships. Relationship rules also differ across cultures. For instance, to some Australian Aboriginal people it is unacceptable to look others straight in the eye. Another example is that in India it is not uncommon for people either to nod *or* shake or to nod *and* shake their heads to mean yes or no. In short, helpers require sensitivity to the body message rules of the social and cultural contexts in which they work as well as to their own and their clients' individual needs.

Helpers require flexibility in making active listening choices that entail bodily communication. As helping relationships develop, clients get to know whether and when their helpers are receptive to them. For instance, clients may know from past experience that when they lean back they are still very attentive. Helpers need to use body messages showing attention and interest selectively. If necessary, they can choose to make their body messages less rewarding: for instance, when they want to check their understanding of what clients say, stop them from rambling on or make points of their own.

Genuineness is important. Both within helpers' body messages and also between helpers' body messages and their voice and verbal messages, consistency increases the chances of clients perceiving them as rewarding listeners. For instance, a helper may smile, yet at the same time either fidget or foot tap. The smile may indicate interest, the fidgeting and foot tapping impatience, and the overall message conveys insincerity. In addition, helpers may make good verbal responses that can be completely negated by poor bodily communication.

ACTIVITIES

Activity 8.1 Raising awareness of good and poor body messages

Your partner talks about a topic of interest to her/him and your role is mainly to listen, however:

- start by using terrible body messages when you respond, then
- switch to using good body messages, then
- hold a debriefing period in which you discuss what it felt like sending and receiving terrible and good body messages.
- Reverse roles and repeat the steps above.

Activity 8.2 Assessing body messages for showing attention and interest

To the extent that they are relevant to the helping setting(s) in which you either use or will use counselling skills, assess yourself on each of the following body messages for showing attention and interest:

- being available;
- adopting a relaxed and open body posture;
- leaning slightly forward;
- using appropriate gaze;
- using appropriate eye contact;
- conveying appropriate facial expressions;
- using good gestures;
- using touch sparingly;

- being sensitive to personal space and height;
- being careful about clothing and grooming;
- cultural considerations in how you communicate with your body; and
- other important areas not listed above.

Activity 8.3 Improving showing attention and interest

Pick a specific body message for showing attention and interest that you think you might improve, for instance, you may have a tendency to sit with too rigid a posture. Then hold a conversation with a partner where you work on improving your chosen body message. Either during or at the end of your conversation ask for feedback on how you are doing.

If appropriate, afterwards you and your partner reverse roles.

9   Paraphrasing and reflecting feelings

The next two somewhat overlapping skills, paraphrasing and reflecting feelings, involve helpers feeding back to clients what they have just communicated. Counselling and helping skills students may wonder 'Why bother?' or think 'Isn't this all rather artificial?' Helper verbalizations of client statements provide rewards for clients to continue. Furthermore, clients' experiences may seem more real to them if they verbalize rather than just think them, and even more real when they then hear these experiences verbalized again by their helpers. Such helper verbalizations may put clients more in touch with their own thoughts, feelings and experiences. Furthermore, by verbalizing what clients communicate, helper and client can engage in a process of exploring and understanding more accurately the meaning of what clients communicate.

Paraphrasing skills

A paraphrase expresses the meaning of a client statement or series of statements in different words. On some occasions, helpers may choose to repeat rather than paraphrase clients' words. For instance, if a client shares a significant insight, it may help the insight sink in if the helper repeats the clients' words. However, more often than not repetition becomes parroting. Clients want to relate to persons, not parrots!

Paraphrasing involves rewording at least the crux of the client's message. Helpers try to convey back to clients clearly and briefly what they have just communicated from their internal frame of reference. When helpers paraphrase, they may sometimes use clients' words, but sparingly. They try to stay close to the kind of language that each client uses. Box 9.1 provides examples of paraphrasing.

Box 9.1 Examples of paraphrasing

Learner to sports professional
Learner: I keep working on my golf swing, but I don't seem to get much better.

Sports professional: Despite your all your efforts, progress is slow, if at all.

Client to probation officer
Client: Last night I bumped into some of my previous mates who tried to tempt me into nicking things again.

Probation officer: Late yesterday your former pals had a go at getting you back into your old ways.

A good paraphrase can provide mirror reflections that are clearer and more succinct than original statements. If so, clients may show appreciation with comments like 'That's right' or 'You've got me'. A simple tip for basic counselling skills students who struggle with paraphrasing is to slow the helping conversation down, thus providing more time to think. Another tip for gaining confidence and fluency is to practice paraphrasing both in and out of class.

Reflecting feelings skills

Most helper responses that reflect feelings are paraphrases that emphasize the emotional content of clients' communications. Reflecting or mirroring feelings is possibly the main skill of active listening. In Chapter 5, I described a five-stage empathy process: listening and observing, resonating, discriminating, communicating and checking. Here I collapse this process into the two stages of identifying feelings and reflecting feelings.

Identifying feelings

Before helpers can reflect a client's feelings back to them, they need to accurately identify or discriminate what they are. Sometimes clients say 'I feel' when they mean 'I think'. For example, 'I feel that equality between the sexes is essential' describes a thought rather than a feeling. On the other hand, 'I feel angry about sex discrimination' describes a feeling. It is important that helpers distinguish between clients' thoughts and feelings if they wish to be skilful at picking up feelings accurately. Following are some ways of identifying feelings.

- *Body messages* Helpers can pick up much about what their client feels from just looking at them. For example, clients may come for help looking tired, worried or happy. They may slump in the chair or sit upright. Sometimes clients send mixed messages in which their body messages are more important than their verbal messages.
- *Vocal messages* Many of the messages about the intensity of clients feelings are conveyed by the degree of vocal emphasis they place on them. Some clients, who are very out of touch with their capacity to feel, may communicate in rather flat and distant voices.
- *Feelings words and phrases* A good but not infallible way to discover what a client feels is to listen to their feelings words and phrases. Feelings words include happy, sad, angry, lonely, anxious, depressed. Feelings phrases are groupings of words that describe feelings. Listening to feelings words may seem a simple guideline, but sometimes basic counselling skills students do not listen carefully enough and then ask clients 'What did you feel?' after clients have just told them.
- *Physical reactions words* Helpers can also identify feelings by listening to clients' physical reactions words. Clients may describe physical reactions with words like tense, tired, pounding heart and headache.
- *Feelings idioms* Feelings idioms are everyday expressions or turns of phrase used to communicate feelings. Very often such idioms are expressed in visual images, but their meaning is so well understood that a helper does not need to conjure up the image to understand the message. For example, 'I'm over the moon' is a feelings idiom describing the emotion of joy.
- *Feelings imagery* Clients can intentionally use visual images to conjure up and communicate feelings. The visual image provides a frame for understanding the feelings content of their messages. For instance, to describe and illustrate embarrassment, clients might use the images of 'I felt like crawling into a corner' or 'I felt like running out of the room'.

Reflecting feelings

A simple guideline for reflecting feelings is to start responses with the personal pronoun 'you' to indicate being 'as if' inside a client's internal frames of reference. When reflecting feelings it is cumbersome always to put 'you feel' before feelings words and phrases. Sometimes 'You're' is sufficient: for example, 'You're delighted' instead of 'You feel delighted'. Even better is to paraphrase and find different words to describe clients' feelings.

Whenever possible, helpers should try to communicate back a client's *main feeling*. Even though clients may not start with their main feeling, they may feel better understood if helpers reflect their main feeling at the front of their response.

Helpers should try to reflect the *strength of feelings*. For instance, after a row, the client may feel 'devastated' (strong feeling), 'upset' (moderate feeling) or 'slightly upset' (weak feeling). Sometimes clients use many words to describe their feelings. The words may cluster around the same theme, in which case one may chose to reflect the crux of the feeling. Alternatively, clients may verbalize varying degrees of *mixed feelings* ranging from simple opposites, for instance, 'happy/sad' to more complex combinations such as 'hurt/anger/guilt'. Good reflections pick up all key elements of feelings messages. On occasion helpers can assist speakers to find the right way to express their feelings. Here reflecting feelings involves helping clients to choose *feelings words that resonate* for them.

Sometimes helpers can reflect clients' *feelings and reasons* that they offer for them. A simple way of doing this is to make a 'You feel . . . because . . .' statement that mirrors their internal frame of reference. Reflecting back reasons does not mean that helpers make an interpretation or offer an explanation from their own perspectives.

It is crucial that helpers *check the accuracy* of their reflections of feelings. Helpers can respond to their clients' feelings statements with differing degrees of tentativeness depending on how clearly the feelings were communicated and how confident they feel about receiving these messages accurately. Almost invariably helpers check by using slightly raised voice inflections towards the end of their responses. On other occasions, helpers can check by asking directly: for instance, 'Do I understand you properly?' Alternatively, helpers may make comments like 'I think I hear you saying (state feelings tentatively) . . .' or 'I want to understand what you're feeling, but I'm still not altogether clear.' Another option is to reflect back a mixed message: for instance, 'On the one hand you are saying you don't mind. On the other hand, you seem tearful.' After a pause the helper might add: 'I'm wondering if you are putting on a brave face?'

An important consideration in reflecting feelings is to understand whether and to what extent clients possess insight into themselves: for example, acknowledging shame, anger, hurt or betrayal. Helpers need to be sensitive about how much reality clients can handle at any given moment in the helping process. Helpers can threaten clients by prematurely or clumsily reflecting feelings that they experience difficulty in acknowledging.

Box 9.2 provides examples of different ways in which helpers can reflect clients' feelings. I do not mean to imply that there is a single correct way of responding to any of the client statements. Reflections of feelings, such as those offered below, can be stepping stones or bridges to clients further experiencing, expressing, exploring and understanding their feelings. Feelings, like ocean waves, are in a constant process of movement. Skilled helpers are able to follow and reflect the ebb and flow of clients' feelings.

Box 9.2 Examples of reflecting feelings

Reflecting feelings words

Client: I'm hopping mad.

Helper: You're furious.

Reflecting feelings phrases

Client: I feel something special between Tom and me.

Helper: You feel that there is mutual attraction . . .

Reflecting physical reactions

Here, if the physical reaction is literally named, there is a case for repetition to show that you have clearly registered it. Otherwise, consider paraphrasing.

Client A: My mouth goes dry.

Helper A: Your mouth goes dry.

Client B: I feel butterflies in my stomach.

Helper B: You feel tension in your stomach.

Searching for feelings that resonate

Client: I don't know how to express my reaction to the way my father treated me . . . possibly angry . . . upset, no that's not quite it . . . bewildered . . .

Helper: Hurt, anxious, confused . . . do any of these words strike a chord?

Reflecting feelings and reasons

Client: Ever since we broke up so unhappily and angrily, I'm afraid to make dates.

Helper: You're scared about dating again because of your really painful break-up.

Small verbal rewards

When assisting clients' to share their internal frames of reference, helpers do not have to reflect every statement that clients make. In addition to using good body message skills, they can use small verbal rewards. Small verbal rewards are brief expressions of helper interest designed to encourage clients to continue talking. The message they convey is 'I am with you. Please go on.' Helpers can use small verbal rewards for good or ill. On the one hand, they can reward clients for sharing and exploring their internal frames of reference. On the other hand, helper use of small verbal rewards may subtly or crudely attempt to shape what clients say. For instance, helpers may reward clients for saying either positive or negative things about themselves. Furthermore, helpers can selectively reward clients for talking about agendas of personal interest to them. Box 9.3 provides some examples of small verbal rewards, though perhaps the most frequently used 'Uh-hum' is more vocal than verbal.

Box 9.3 Examples of small verbal rewards

'Uh-hum.'	'Sure.'
'Please continue.'	'Indeed.'

'Tell me more.'	'And . . .'
'Go on.'	'So . . .'
'I see.'	'Really.'
'Oh?'	'Right.'
'Then . . .'	'Yes.'
'I hear you.'	

Open-ended questions

In addition to reflecting feelings and small verbal rewards, helpers may use open-ended questions in ways that help clients to elaborate their internal frames of reference. Such questions allow clients to share their internal viewpoints without curtailing their options. A good use of open-ended questions is when, in the initial session, helpers wish to assist clients to say why they have come. In subsequent sessions, too, helpers are likely to find open-ended questions useful. Open-ended questions include: 'Tell me about it?', 'Please elaborate?' and, slightly less open-ended, 'How do you feel about that?'

Open-ended questions may be contrasted with closed questions that curtail speakers' options: indeed, they often give only two options, 'yes' or 'no'.

Open-ended question: How was your day?
Closed questions: Was your day good or bad?
  What did you do today?

I am not suggesting that helpers never use closed questions. It depends on the goals of their listening. Furthermore, many helpers have to ask closed questions to perform other primary roles. Closed questions can be essential for collecting information. However, helpers should show restraint when they wish to help others share their worlds on their own terms.

ACTIVITIES

Activity 9.1 Paraphrasing skills

1   Go to Box 9.1 on page 57 and provide at least one alternative paraphrase to each of the two client statements.
2   Working in a pair, each partner 'feeds' one another's statements. Listeners paraphrase speakers' statements and speakers provide feedback on their reactions to each paraphrase. One option is for partners to alternate roles after each statement-response-feedback unit.

Activity 9.2 Reflecting feelings skills

1   Reproduce Box 9.2 from pages 60–1, providing your own examples of helpers reflecting their clients' feelings in each of these areas:
   •   reflecting feelings words;
   •   reflecting feelings phrases;
   •   reflecting physical reactions;
   •   searching for feelings that resonate; and
   •   reflecting feelings and reasons.
2   Work with a partner. Each person takes turns to be speaker and listener. The speaker picks a topic about which she/he feels comfortable sharing her/his feelings. When listening, help the speaker to talk about her/his feelings by reflecting them accurately. When both listening and responding, pay attention to vocal and body messages as well as to verbal messages.

10 Starting and structuring

Good beginnings increase the chances of good middles and good endings. Poor beginnings can either lose clients or lose ground in helping that may then be hard to retrieve. Whether in informal or formal settings, helpers can start the helping process in friendly and functional ways. The appropriate way to start helping varies according to the different roles that helpers play. Helpers using counselling skills as part of other roles or in informal settings will need to adjust to their own circumstances some of the skills suggested here for starting helping.

Permissions to talk

Permissions to talk are brief statements inviting clients to tell their stories and indicating that helpers are prepared to listen. Permissions to talk are 'door openers' that give clients the message 'I'm interested and prepared to listen. Please share with me your internal frame of reference.' Helpers are there to discover information about clients and to assist clients to discover information about themselves.

Helping students and helpers should be careful about using common opening remarks like 'How can I help you?' or 'What can I do for you? Such remarks can get initial sessions off to unfortunate starts by suggesting that clients are dependent on helpers' resources rather than on developing their own resources for later self-help.

When giving clients permission to talk, helpers' body and vocal messages are very important in indicating that they are comfortable and trustworthy people with whom to talk. Helpers should try to create a safe emotional climate. Speaking clearly and relatively slowly may help to create a calm environment. Helpers should also use appropriate body messages for showing attention and interest, an area already reviewed in Chapter 8.

Many readers have informal contacts with clients outside of formal helping sessions, for instance, correctional officers in facilities for delinquents, residential staff in half-way houses for former drug addicts, or nurses in hospitals. Here helpers may use permissions to talk when they sense that someone has a personal agenda that bothers them, but requires that extra bit of encouragement to share it. Box 10.1 provides some suggestions for permissions to talk for use in both formal and informal helping. In addition, I include some follow up statements that helpers can use when they become aware that their clients are finding it difficult to get started.

Box 10.1 Examples of permissions to talk

Formal settings

Please tell me why you've come?

Please tell me what brings you here?

Please tell me what's concerning you?

Please tell me what's the problem?

Please put me in the picture?

Where would you like to start?

You've been referred by _____. Now how do you see your situation?

Informal settings

Is there something on your mind?

I'm available if you want to talk.

You seem unhappy today (said sympathetically).

Follow up 'lubricating' comments

It's pretty hard to get started.

Take your time.

When you're ready.

Sometimes, helpers may need to complete organizational requirements for gathering basic information before giving clients permission
to talk. However, be flexible: for instance, clients in crisis require psychological comfort before bureaucratic form filling which can come
later. On occasion, helpers may need to indicate the limitations of confidentiality surrounding the session, such as the need to report to a
third party or any legal limitations. In addition, helpers who take notes
may offer brief initial explanations for so doing or even ask clients'
permission.

Some counselling skills students and helpers need to record helping
sessions for supervision purposes. On many courses, clients who see
students under supervision know in advance that their sessions will be
recorded. If this is not the case, permission to record will need to be
sought right at the start of the session. Box 10.2 provides an example of
requesting permission from a client to record. In addition, good body
and vocal messages can make it easier to obtain permission. Students
and helpers who ask permission in nervous and hesitant ways are
more likely to trigger doubts and resistances in clients than those
asking calmly and confidently.

Box 10.2 Example of a request to record a session

Would you mind if I videotaped this session for supervision purposes? Only my supervisor [if relevant add 'and supervision group']
will see the tape which will be scrubbed clean when it has been
reviewed. If you want, we can turn the recorder off at any time.

Summarizing skills

Summaries are brief helper statements about longer excerpts from helping sessions. Summaries pull together, clarify and reflect back different

parts of a series of client statements either during a discussion unit, at the end of a discussion unit or at the beginning or end of helping sessions.

Here I focus on helper summaries at the start of helping. Where possible, helper summaries serve to move the session forward. Such summaries may mirror back to clients segments of what they have said, check and clarify understanding or identify themes, problem areas and problem situations. Summaries may serve other purposes as well. If clients have had a lengthy period of talking, helpers can summarize to establish their presence and make the helping conversation more two-way. Furthermore, if clients tell their stories very rapidly, helpers may deliver summaries at a measured speech rate to calm clients down.

When clients tell why they have come for helping, helpers may use summaries that reflect whole units of communication. Such summaries tie together the main feelings and content of what clients say. Basic reflection summaries serve a bridging function for clients enabling them to continue with the same topic or move on to another. Other functions include making sure helpers listen accurately, rewarding clients and clarifying both parties' understanding. A variation of the basic reflection summary is the reflecting feelings and reasons summary that links emotions with their perceived causes.

Another useful summarizing skill for early in helping is to be able to provide an overview of different problem areas. Imagine that a client comes to seek your assistance and starts describing a number of different problems. Identification of problem area summaries can provide clients with clearer statements than they managed on their own. Furthermore, such summaries can provide a basis for asking clients to prioritize either which problem is most important or where they want to focus first. Box 10.3 provides examples of summarizing statements.

Box 10.3 Examples of summaries

Basic reflection summary

Helper to terminal cancer patient

You feel better now that the doctor has told you that he should always be able to control your pain. You've been so used to looking after your family that it's a real shock to realize that your illness means that you will have progressively less energy to do so much for them in future. You hate having to be dependent on other people, especially your children. You also want to gather your thoughts together regarding how best to use the remainder of your life.

Identification of problem areas summary

Welfare worker to young person

As I see it you have described at least four problems to me. One is the problem of getting somewhere decent to live at a price you can afford. Another problem is how to stop arguing with your boyfriend so frequently. Still another problem is how to keep in touch with your family and yet not get dominated by them when you do see them. Last, you are unhappy only getting casual work and want to see if you can do a course to improve your employment prospects. Is that a fair summary?

Structuring skills

Helping sessions are new experiences for many clients. Helpers can try to make the helping process more comprehensible and less threatening. Structuring entails explaining the helping process to clients. Helpers communicate structure by body and vocal as well as by verbal messages. Here I only review structuring during the first part of helping, which may only last the first 10 to 15 minutes of an initial session. It is probably best to structure in two statements, an opening statement and a follow-up statement, rather than do it all at the beginning. If helpers offer the whole explanation at the beginning, they may fail to respond to clients who want emotional release or are desperate to share information.

In two-part structuring, helpers' opening statements provide the first occasion for structuring. Here they can establish time boundaries and give clients permission to talk. After helpers have used their active listening skills to assist clients to say why they have come, they may summarize the main points for clients and check the accuracy of their summaries. Then helpers briefly and simply explain the remainder of the helping process to clients. Box 10.4 presents two follow-up structuring statements providing a framework for the Relating–Understanding–Changing helping model presented in Chapter 6. The first statement is where the client clearly has only one main problem and the second statement is where the client has presented with more than one problem. If a specific situation has not already emerged, a helper's follow-up statement requests the client to identify a situation within a main problem area for their work together.

Box 10.4 Examples of structuring statements

Opening or first structuring statement
We have about 40 minutes together, please tell me why you've come?

Possible second structuring statements
1 Single problem
You've given me some idea why you have come. Now since time is limited, I wonder if together we can select a specific situation within your problem [specify] that we can work on. I will help you to understand the situation more fully and then we can examine strategies for dealing better with it. Is that OK with you?

2 More than one problem
After summarizing the different problem areas, the helper says:

Which of these would you like to focus on? [The client states her or his choice.] Good. Now I wonder if we can identify a particular situation within this problem that it is important for you to manage better. Then we can explore this situation more fully and perhaps come up with some useful strategies for dealing with it. Is that all right with you?

Structuring can strengthen collaborative working relationships by establishing agendas or goals for the helping process as well as obtaining agreement on how to proceed. Helpers may need to help clients choose a particular situation to work on that is important for them. Helpers may also need to respond to questions. However, helpers should not allow themselves to be lured into an intellectual discussion of the helping process. If they make structuring statements in a comfortable and confident way, most clients will be happy to work within the suggested framework.

ACTIVITIES

Activity 10.1 Starting and structuring

Work with a partner. Each of you thinks of a specific problem situation in your personal or work life that you are prepared to share in role-playing the beginning of an initial session. Alternatively, you can role-play a client with a genuine problem situation. One of you acts as client. The helper conducts an interview of up to 15 minutes using the following skills:

- making an opening statement;
- giving permission to talk;
- paraphrasing;
- reflecting feelings;
- using small rewards;
- using open-ended questions;
- summarizing; and
- making a second structuring statement.

By the end of this beginning section of the session, the helper should have assisted the client in identifying a specific situation for your future work together.

After completing the first part of an initial helping session, conduct a review together, possibly illustrated by going through a videotape or audio-cassette of the session.

Then, after a suitable interval, partners can reverse roles.

11 Asking questions

In most instances, when helpers ask questions arising from other roles, for instance, the role of social worker, doctor, financial adviser or lawyer, questions relevant to their primary tasks are inevitable. This chapter on asking questions focuses mainly on asking questions where the clients' problems have a large psychological component to them. There is a great danger that, when helpers question clients, they revert to previous modes of relating and lose some if not all of their active listening skills. Helpers should rein in tendencies to question too much and listen too little. In addition, helpers should be mindful that if they can create safe emotional climates, clients will reveal more and deeper information, often without having to be asked.

Questions have the potential to damage helping relationships, sometimes beyond repair. Clients can resent being interrogated from helpers' frames of reference rather than being understood from their own. For example, insufficiently skilled helpers may ask a series of questions, scarcely listen to the answers and then go off on another tangent whether or not clients see this as relevant. In addition, clients resent intrusive questioning about sensitive personal material. Furthermore, by clumsily taking control, helpers can create resistances and anger. Even if clients appear acquiescent, helpers may have encouraged their dependency rather than helping them assume responsibility for their lives.

How do helpers go about assisting clients to clarify and expand their understanding of problem situations? Without becoming too regimented, helper and client engage in a process of systematic inquiry about different aspects or 'angles' of a situation. However, when learning how to question, I encourage basic counselling skills students to err on the side of asking too few rather than too many questions. Once they are more skilled at asking a few well-chosen questions within the context of collaborative working relationships, then they can gradually build up the number of questions they ask, but never to the point where they control and de-power clients.

How helpers question is very important in addition to what they say. When questioning, helpers should use good vocal messages in terms of volume, articulation, pitch, emphasis and speech rate. For example, clients may feel overwhelmed if helpers' voices are loud and harsh. Furthermore, helpers' body messages should clearly show their attention and interest in clients' answers. For instance, if helpers use little eye contact and have a stiff body posture, clients may feel less inclined to answer questions well.

Questions about feelings and physical reactions

Questions can assist clients in being specific about feelings and physical reactions. Frequently, since helpers cannot assume a common meaning, they need to clarify the labels that clients attach to feelings. For instance, follow-up questions to a client who says 'I am very depressed' might be: 'When you say you are very depressed, what exactly do you mean?' or 'When you say you are very depressed what are your specific feelings and physical reactions?' or 'You feel very depressed. Tell me more about that feeling?' Then the helper can collaborate with the client to identify the relevant feelings and physical reactions. Sometimes helpers may directly check out specific feelings or physical reactions, for instance 'Do you feel suicidal sometimes?' or 'How is your appetite?'

Helpers often need to assist clients in expanding and elaborating their feelings and physical reactions. Box 11.1 provides some illustrative questions.

Box 11.1 Examples of questions that focus on feelings and physical reactions

When did you start feeling this way?

Tell me more about the feeling?

Describe how your body experiences the feeling?

Do you have any visual images that capture the feeling?

How has your mood been and how is it today?

Are there any other feelings that accompany or underlie that feeling?

How do you feel here and now?

How persistent is the feeling?

On a scale of 0 to 10 (or 0 to 100) how strong is the feeling?

Questions about thinking

Helpers can assist clients to reveal their thoughts by asking appropriate questions. One approach to asking questions about thinking is called 'Think aloud'. Think aloud involves encouraging clients to speak aloud their thought processes in relation to specific situations. For instance, clients can be asked to take helpers in slow motion through their thoughts and feelings in relation to specific anxiety-evoking experiences.

Sometimes helpers can access thinking from feelings, for instance 'What thoughts preceded or accompanied those feelings?' On other occasions helpers may choose to access thinking from a client's or from another person's behaviour, for example 'When you did that what were you thinking?' or 'When she/he said that, what went through your mind?' Helpers can also ask follow-up questions such as 'Were there any other thoughts or images?'

Another way to look at thoughts is in terms of their strength. One way to do this is to label thoughts as cool, warm and hot. In particular helpers assist clients to look out for hot thoughts that may trigger unwanted feelings and self-defeating communications. Often, clients' thoughts about what other people are thinking can be the hot thoughts that drive their poor communication, for example, following the thought 'She/he is out to get me' with an angry outburst against her/him. Box 11.2 provides some illustrative questions focusing on clients' thinking.

Box 11.2 Examples of questions focusing on thinking

What thoughts did you have before/during/after the situation?

What was going through your mind just before you started to feel this way?

What images do you get in the situation?

Go in slow motion through your thoughts in the situation?

How frequently do you get those thoughts?

When she/he acted like that, what did you think?

Which of those thoughts is the hot thought?

What do you think she/he was thinking?

What are you afraid of?

What resources or strengths do you have in the situation?

What memories is this situation stirring up?

Were there any other thoughts or images?

In addition, helpers can ask specific questions about self-talk, rules and perceptions.

Helpers can assist clients to understand how they can think more deeply if they go beyond facts to search for their interpretations and perceptions. The information clients provide often has personal or symbolic meaning for them. For example, partners who do not receive flowers on their birthday may or may not think that this symbolizes lack of love. Questions that probe for personal meanings should be open and tentative since clients should know the answers better than anyone else, even if this does not always seem to be the case. Illustrative questions include: 'I'm wondering what the meaning of . . . is for you?', 'What do you make of that?' and 'Why is . . . so important for you?'

Questions about communications and actions

Questions about clients' communication and actions aim to elicit specific details of how they behave. Often clients' reports are vague and they require assistance in becoming more specific. Sometimes helpers are poor at assisting clients to discover what actually happened in situations and so the vagueness persists. Box 11.3 provides some examples of questions focusing on communication and actions.

Box 11.3 Examples of questions focusing on communication/actions

How did you behave?

What did you/I say?

How were you communicating with your voice?

How were you communicating with your body language?

How did she/he react when you did that [specify]?

What is the pattern of communication that develops between you when you row?

What happened before you did that?

What were the consequences of doing that?

When do you communicate that way?

Where do you act that way?

How many times a day/week/month do you . . .?

How many minutes/hours do you . . . each day?

A further question focusing on communications and actions is 'Show me?' Clients can be invited to illustrate the verbal, vocal and body messages they used in an interaction either on their own or in a role-play with the helper playing the other party. For instance, teachers having difficulty disciplining children can show the counsellor how they attempt to do this. Role-play allows the possibility of exploring patterns of communication that extend beyond an initial 'show me' response focused on just one unit of interaction. Helpers can also videorecord role-plays and play them back to clients to illustrate points and develop clients' skills of observing themselves.

Interspersing active listening with questions

Clients feel interrogated when helpers ask a series of questions in quick succession. Helpers can greatly soften their questioning if they pause to see if clients wish to continue responding and then reflect each response. Interspersing active listening has the added advantage of ensuring that helpers check the accuracy of their understanding. Box 11.4 illustrates the process of interspersing active listening with questions. In this excerpt, the helper facilitates Beth's description of her internal frame of reference and encourages her to reveal her feelings and physical reactions.

Box 11.4 Interspersing active listening with questions

Problem situation
Beth, a 34 year-old mature student, comes to her helper worried about failing her undergraduate psychology course. The particular situation that she chooses to focus on is a statistics exam that is coming up in two weeks time.

Interspersing active listening with questions

Beth: I'm getting very anxious over my statistics exam in two weeks time.

Helper: You're increasingly worried about your stats exam . . . Can you tell me more about how you're experiencing your anxiety?

Beth: Yes, I get tense just thinking about it, especially in my chest.

Helper: Tension in your chest . . . how bad is this on a scale of 0 to 10?

Beth:	It fluctuates. It started around 2 or 3, but as the exam gets closer, sometimes it's 7 or 8.
Helper:	So the tension is getting really uncomfortable. Are there any other feelings or physical reactions connected with the exam?
Beth:	I'm not sleeping well and I'm listless much of the time. I've never felt this anxious about exams before.
Helper:	It's really getting to you and affecting your sleep and energy level too.

Helpers should always listen carefully to and respect what clients have just said. Frequently, their next question can follow on from and encourage clients to build upon their last response. Questioning that is logically linked to clients' responses creates a feeling of working together rather than of being directed by helpers. At the end of asking questions to clarify a problem situation, helpers can summarize the main points and check with clients about the accuracy and completeness of their summaries.

ACTIVITIES

Activity 11.1 Assessing and formulating questions

1   Look at Box 11.1 on pages 72–3.
   • Which questions do you think are really useful for probing clients' feelings and physical reactions?
   • Can you think of other useful questions that helpers might ask for this purpose?
2   Look at Box 11.2 on page 74.
   • Which questions do you think are really useful for probing clients' thinking?
   • Can you think of other useful questions that helpers might ask for this purpose?
3   Look at Box 11.3 on page 75.
   • Which questions do you think are really useful for probing clients' communications and actions?
   • Can you think of other useful questions that helpers might ask for this purpose?

Activity 11.2 Interspersing active listening with questions

Work with a partner.

- Each partner picks a problem situation.
- Partner A acts as helper and Partner B acts as client.
- Partner A spends 10 to 15 minutes interspersing questions with active listening as together she/he clarifies Problem B's problem situation by asking questions about:
  - feelings and physical reactions;
  - thinking;
  - communication and actions; and
  - anything else she/he considers relevant.
- At the end Partner A summarizes the main details covered so far.
- Hold a sharing and feedback session.
- Afterwards, if feasible, reverse roles and repeat the activity.

12   Monitoring

In addition to using active listening skills and asking questions, in some settings helpers can assist clients to clarify problems by monitoring their feelings, physical reactions, thoughts and communications/actions. Helpers may need explain to clients why monitoring can be useful. Systematic monitoring can be important at the start of, during and after helping. At the outset, systematic monitoring can establish baselines and increase awareness. During helping, monitoring can serve to remind, check on progress and motivate. After helping, monitoring is relevant to maintaining gains, though clients may not be so systematic in collecting information as during helping. Here I focus on monitoring at the start of helping.

Monitoring feelings and physical reactions

Helpers can encourage clients to monitor their feelings and physical reactions by using brief rating scales either daily or in terms of specific situations. Clients can be asked to rate themselves on feelings such as mood (very happy to very depressed), anxiety level (no anxiety to very anxious), feelings of stress (no stress to very stressed) and so on. Common rating scales range from 0–10 or 0–100. Helpers may need to train clients in the skills of identifying and rating the key or important feelings and physical reactions they experience either daily or in situations. On the next page is an example of a simple scale that clients can use to rate their level or anxiety either for each day or for specific situations.

No anxiety 0 1 2 3 4 5 6 7 8 9 10 **Extremely anxious**

Helpers can also assist clients to use worksheets to monitor and become more aware of how they feel in specific situations. Box 12.1 shows such a worksheet filled out in conjunction with a client in a difficult relationship with a boss at work. Helpers need to give clients some practice in filling out such worksheets before asking them to complete them on their own.

Box 12.1 Worksheet for identifying and rating key feelings, physical reactions and thoughts in a situation

Situation
(Who? What? When? Where?)

Friday, 5.30 p.m.

I'm working late and my boss says 'Haven't you finished that job yet?'

Key feeling(s) and physical reaction(s)
(What did I feel? How did I physically react? Rating for each key feeling and physical reaction (0–100%).)

Angry   80%

Hurt   60%

Tense   65%

Thoughts (perceptions and images)
(What thoughts did I have just before I started to feel and physically react this way? Place a star by any hot thoughts.)

She/he is angry with me.

*I don't need this extra hassle on top of the pressure I already feel.

I was looking forward to getting home.

I am being treated like a machine.

My boss promises customers too much too soon, which puts unnecessary pressure on the staff.

Monitoring thinking

Helpers can encourage clients to monitor their thoughts, perceptions and images. Sometimes such monitoring is in conjunction with monitoring feelings and physical reactions as well (see Box 12.1). Clients can be asked to put a star by any hot thoughts most associated with the feelings and physical reactions. Another approach to monitoring thoughts is to ask clients to count every time they get a specific self-defeating thought, for instance 'I'm no good'. Counting can help clients to become aware of the repetitive nature of their thinking. Clients may then record over a period of time the daily frequency of targeted thoughts and perceptions.

A further approach to monitoring thinking is to use the Situation–Thoughts–Consequences (STC) framework which can be used by helpers and clients alike as a tool for analysing how thoughts mediate between situations and how clients feel, physically react, communicate and act about them. In this framework:

S = Situation (situations that clients face)
T = Thoughts (thoughts and visual images)
C = Consequences (feelings, physical reactions, communications and actions)

The idea is that clients do not go automatically from the situation (S) to the consequences of the situation (C). Instead the consequences (C) of the situation (S) are mediated by what and how they think (T). Their feelings, physical reactions, communications and actions, for good or ill, are mediated by their thoughts and mental processes.

Box 12.2 provides an STC worksheet that clients can use both to monitor and analyse their thoughts in situations. Helpers need to show clients how to complete the worksheet. I have filled out the worksheet for Tricia, a 35 year-old who is very anxious about a forthcoming job interview and thinks in negative ways.

Box 12.2 STC (Situation–Thoughts–Consequences) worksheet

Situation
State my problem situation clearly and succinctly.

In one week's time I have an important job interview.

Thoughts
Record my thoughts about the situation.

I must do very well.

I'm no good at job interviews.

I am afraid that I will fail.

Consequences
What are the consequences of my thoughts about the situation?

My feelings and physical reactions:

* Feelings: very anxious.
* Physical reactions: tension in my stomach, not sleeping properly.

My communications and actions

* In the past I have been very wooden in interviews.
* I play it safe rather than take the risk of applying for challenging and better paid jobs.

Monitoring communication and actions

Helpers can encourage clients to monitor their behaviour and so become more aware of how they communicate and act in problem areas. Sometimes clients agree to perform homework tasks, for instance, telephoning to ask for a date and then recording how they behaved. The following are methods by which helpers can encourage clients to monitor how they communicate and act.

Diaries and journals

Keeping a diary or journal is one way of monitoring communications and actions. Clients can pay special attention to writing up critical incidents where they have used good or poor behaviours. Although diaries and journals may be useful, some clients find this approach all too easy to ignore and too unsystematic.

Frequency charts

Frequency charts focus on how many times clients enact a specific behaviour in a given time period, be it daily, weekly or monthly. For example, clients may tally up how many cigarettes they smoke in a day and then transfer this information to a monthly chart broken down by days. Another example is that of unemployed Tuan who agrees with his employment counsellor to record, each day for a week, his job search behaviours on a Job Search Activity Chart. The chart lists activities on the horizontal axis and days on the vertical axis. The activities listed on the horizontal axis are written application, phone application, letter enquiry, phone enquiry, cold canvas, approach to contact, employment centre visit and interview attended. The counsellor instructs Tuan to write the number 1 in the relevant box each time he performs an action.

Situation–thoughts–consequences (STC) logs

Filling in the three-part situation–thoughts–consequences (STC) logs or worksheets can help clients to see the connections between how they think and how they felt, physically reacted and communicated or acted. See Box 12.2 for an example.

Verbal, vocal and body message logs

Frequently clients possess a low awareness of their vocal and body communication. During the understanding stage, helpers and clients may become aware of some areas important for understanding clients' problem situations. For instance, a helper works with Malcolm, a married man with three children, whose problem situations centre around his difficulty setting limits on his widowed mother, Freya, who makes repeated telephone and face-to-face requests for time and attention, even though she is well able to look after herself. Box 12.3 shows a log to collect information about how Malcolm communicates in these situations. Malcolm is cued in advance to observe specific verbal, vocal and body messages.

Assisting clients to monitor

Clients are not in the habit of systematically recording observations about how they feel, physically react, think and communicate/act. Helpers may need to motivate them to do so. For instance, a helper

---

Box 12.3 Example of verbal, vocal and body message log

Situation	How I communicated		
	Verbal messages	Vocal messages	Body messages
1			
2 (and so on)			

---

could explain to Malcolm: 'Systematically writing down how you communicate with your words, voice and body each time your mother attempts to get you to go over to her place provides us with information to develop useful strategies for setting limits on her dependent behaviour.'

Helpers should always either supply monitoring logs or supervise clients in setting up the format for a log. Helpers should not expect clients to make logs on their own. Clients may not do so in the first place and, if they do, they may get them wrong.

Clients are not naturally accurate self-observers. Consequently, helpers may need to train them in discriminating and recording specific behaviours. Clients require clarity not only about what to record, but also about how to record it. In addition, they require an awareness of any tendencies they have to misperceive or selectively perceive their actions: for instance, being more inclined to notice weaknesses than strengths.

Helpers should reward clients with interest and praise when they fill in logs. This guideline is based on the basic behavioural principle that actions that are rewarding are more likely to be repeated. Furthermore, helpers should always reward clients for their efforts by debriefing them. Helpers can encourage clients to use information they record on monitoring logs for self-exploration and evaluation. Without doing their work for them, helpers can help clients to understand the meaning of the information they have collected.

ACTIVITIES

Activity 12.1 Monitoring feelings, physical reactions and thoughts

Role-play helping a partner who acts as a 'client' and has a specific situation in which she/he is experiencing feelings and physical reactions that may be self-defeating. Offer reasons to your client for monitoring her/his feelings, physical reactions and thoughts. Using the format of Box 12.1 on page 80, help your client to identify key feelings, physical reactions and thoughts in the situation.

Afterwards, hold a feedback and discussion session. Then, if appropriate, reverse roles.

Activity 12.2 Monitoring situations, thoughts and consequences

Role-play helping a partner who acts as a 'client' and has a specific situation in which she/he is behaving in a self-defeating manner. Offer reasons to your client for monitoring to discover the relationship between her/his thoughts, feelings and communications/actions. Using the STC format of Box 12.2 on pages 81–2, help your client to describe the situation and to identify her/his thinking, and the feelings/physical reactions and communication/actions consequences.

Afterwards, hold a feedback and discussion session. Then, if appropriate, reverse roles.

Activity 12.3 Monitoring verbal, vocal and body messages

Role-play helping a partner who acts as a 'client' and has a specific situation in which she/he either is or may be communicating poorly. Offer reasons to your client for monitoring her/his communication in the situation. Then, using the format of the log in Box 12.3 on page 84, train your client to observe and record systematically her/his verbal, vocal and body messages in the situation.

Afterwards, hold a feedback and discussion session. Then, if appropriate, reverse roles.

13   Offering challenges and feedback

This chapter differs from previous chapters in that the skills of offering challenges and offering feedback represent responses more clearly emanating from the helper's external frame of reference than designed to clarify the client's internal frame of reference. The starting point of any good collaborative working relationship is to use active listening and asking questions skills to understand and clarify the client's frame of reference. Offering challenges and offering feedback are two skills that helpers can use that go beyond clarifying clients' existing frames of references to expand how they view themselves and their problems.

Offering challenges

'Challenging' is perhaps a more gentle word than 'confronting', which conjures up images of clients sitting in hot seats having their self-protective habits remorselessly stripped away by aggressive helpers. Challenges come from helpers' external frames of reference with the aim of helping clients to develop new and better perspectives about themselves, others and their problem situations. Skilfully crafted challenges invite clients to examine discrepancies in their feelings, thoughts and communications about which, for various reasons, they remain insufficiently aware. The challenges I advocate here have two distinctive characteristics: first, they tend to be fairly close to clients' existing internal frames of reference; and second they are given in a relatively non-threatening manner. As Box 13.1 illustrates, challenges can come in many shapes and sizes.

Box 13.1 Examples of challenging inconsistencies

Inconsistency between verbal, vocal and/or body messages
You're telling me you feel nervous right now, yet you are smiling.

Inconsistency between words and actions
You say that you really love her, but that you are also so engaged in your business that you can hardly find time to see her.

Inconsistency between values and actions
You say you believe in equality between the sexes, but you also feel uncomfortable about letting a woman pick up the tab.

Inconsistency between giving and keeping one's word
On the one hand you said that you would contact her/him this past week, yet somehow you keep finding reasons for not doing so.

Inconsistency between earlier and present statements
Last session you said you really liked your father-in-law, now you're saying that he's a pretty difficult person to be around.

Inconsistency between statements and evidence
You said your oldest son never appreciates you, but now you've just told me that he took you out to dinner on your birthday.

Inconsistency between own and others' evaluations
I'm getting two messages. You feel that you are trusting and not jealous, but the feedback from your girlfriend seems to be that you keep jumping to conclusions and interpreting her actions negatively.

How to offer challenges

Verbal messages for offering challenges include: 'On the one hand . . . on the other . . .', 'On the one hand . . . but . . .'; 'You say . . . but . . .' and 'I'm getting two messages . . .' or 'I'm getting a mixed message . . .' Helpers' vocal and body messages should remain relaxed and friendly. Beginning helpers should restrict themselves to offering no more than mildly threatening challenges to clients because of the huge potential for helping relationships to turn sour when inexperienced helpers make strong challenges.

When challenging, it is important to keep clients' ears open to the new information. Therefore, helpers should offer their challenges as equals, avoid talking down to clients and always remember that challenges are invitations for exploration. A major risk in challenging clients is that they perceive what helpers say as put-downs.

Helpers should use a minimum amount of 'muscle', only offering challenges as strongly as their goals require. Strong challenges can create resistances. Although sometimes necessary, even with skilled helpers such challenges are generally best avoided. This is especially so early in helping relationships when rapport and trust are not yet established. Strategies that clients can use to resist challenges include discrediting challengers, persuading challengers to change their views, devaluing the issue, seeking support elsewhere for views being challenged, and agreeing with the challenge inside helping but then doing nothing about it outside.

Helpers should leave the ultimate responsibility for assessing the value of their challenges with clients, who can then decide whether the challenges actually help them to move forward in their explorations. Often challenges are only mildly discrepant to clients' existing perceptions. If well timed and tactfully worded, such challenges are unlikely to elicit a high degree of defensiveness.

Lastly, helpers should be careful not to overdo offering challenges. Nobody likes being persistently challenged. With constant challenges helpers create unsafe emotional climates. If they offer challenges skillfully, they can help clients to enlarge their understanding and act more effectively. However, if helpers challenge too often and too clumsily, they can block clients from achieving insight and undermine the creation of good collaborative working relationships.

Offering feedback

Offering feedback skills and offering challenges skills overlap. However, challenging skills are used in response to clients' inconsistencies, whereas there is no assumption of inconsistency in this section on offering feedback skills. Here I distinguish between observational feedback, 'I observe you as . . .', and experiential feedback, ' I experience you as . . .'.

Observational feedback

Helpers as observers of clients' communication may see it differently, and possibly more accurately, than clients perceive it themselves. When helpers and clients are truly collaborating to try and understand clients' problems and problem situations, there might be occasions where helpers may decide to offer feedback to clients based on their own observations. Take clients who have just shown helpers how they communicate in specific situations. After mini role-plays, clients may show some insight into their verbal, vocal and body messages. However, as observers, helpers may wish to bring something else to their attention.

How do helpers go about offering feedback to clients? Box 13.2 makes many suggestions about how helpers can go about this task. These suggestions include: using 'I' messages; being specific and, where possible, stating feedback in the positive; using confirmatory as well as corrective feedback; considering demonstrating feedback; and providing opportunities for clients to respond to feedback.

Box 13.2 Guidelines for offering feedback

Use 'I' messages rather than 'You' messages
'You' message:

You did . . .

'I' message:

I thought you . . .

Be specific and, where possible, state feedback in the positive
Non specific and negative:

You performed poorly.

Specific and positive:

I thought you could use more eye contact and speak in a louder voice.

Use confirmatory as well as corrective feedback
I thought your use of eye contact was good, but that you could still speak in a louder voice.

Consider emotional as well as behavioural feedback

When you made very direct eye contact and spoke in a loud voice, I felt overpowered by you.

Consider demonstrating feedback

I would like to show you how your eye contact came over to me . . . [then demonstrate].

Provide opportunities for clients to respond to feedback

What's your reaction to what I've just said?

After conducting mini role-plays, my preference is to ask clients to evaluate themselves before offering any feedback. Reasons for doing this include encouraging clients to participate actively and reducing the need for feedback from me since clients may have noticed my points anyway. Further reasons are to build clients' skills of self-observation and to increase the likelihood of their being receptive to my feedback because they have already been given the opportunity to assess themselves. For instance, after inviting clients to comment on their performance and listening to their responses, I might summarize what they have said, enquire 'Would you mind if I make one or two observations . . .?' and then, if given permission, succinctly offer my feedback.

Experiential feedback

Feedback can also involve helpers in using their experiencing of clients as springboards for offering observations about both the client and the helping process. To an extent, helping sessions and contacts can be microcosms of outside life. Clients can bring into them the same patterns of communication that create difficulties for them outside helping. However, helpers should be very careful not to let their own personal unfinished business interfere with how they experience clients.

Instances where helpers' experiencing of clients' interpersonal style may throw light on their problems outside include not coming on time for interviews, speaking in distant ways and seeking reassurance. For instance, with a client who continually seeks reassurance, a helper might comment: 'I am put on the spot because I experience pressure from you for reassurance, whereas I'd like to encourage you to rely on your own judgements.' Giving positive experiential feedback to clients with low self-esteem can sometimes be helpful, for example, 'I experience you as having some strength to deal with the situation' or 'I experience you as having much to offer a friend'. Such comments need to be genuine feedback rather than superficial reassurance.

Helpers can also offer experiential feedback concerning the helping process. For example, if clients repetitively go over the same ground, the helper might say: 'I experience you as having taken that topic as far as you can go at the moment and it might be profitable to move on. What do you think?' Another example is that of the helper who shares how she or he experiences a client who uses humour as a distancing device whenever topics become too personal. For instance, the helper could comment 'I get the sense that this topic is getting too close for comfort and so you're starting to act the clown to avoid dealing with it directly.' Needless to say, tact and good timing is very important if clients are to use such experiential feedback to move forwards rather than backwards.

ACTIVITIES

Activity 13.1 Offering challenges skills

1 What does the concept of offering challenges to clients mean to you? Early in a helping relationship, what are the advantages and disadvantages of offering challenges to clients?
2 Using Box 13.1 on page 87 as a guide, formulate a challenging response in each of the following areas:
   • inconsistency between verbal, vocal and/or body messages;
   • inconsistency between words and actions;
   • inconsistency between values and actions;
   • inconsistency between giving and keeping one's word;
   • inconsistency between earlier and present statements;
   • inconsistency between statements and evidence; and
   • inconsistency between own and others' evaluations.

Activity 13.2 Offering feedback skills

1 Refer to the guidelines for offering feedback in Box 13.2 on pages 89–90 and formulate statements for illustrating each of the different guidelines.
2 Work in a pair with Partner A as 'client' and Partner B as 'helper'.
   • Partner A selects a problem situation involving another person where she/he thinks she/he might communicate better.

- Partners A and B conduct a mini role-play in which Partner B plays the other person and Partner A demonstrates how she/he currently communicates in the situation.
- Afterwards, Partner B invites Partner A to comment on her/his verbal, vocal and body messages in the situation. Then Partner B gives observational feedback to Partner A.
- Next, hold a sharing and discussion session about Partner A's offering observational feedback skills.
- Then, if appropriate reverse roles.

3 What does the concept of offering experiential feedback mean to you?
4 Formulate one or more offering experiential feedback statements.

14 Self-disclosing

Helpers relate to clients in numerous settings, formal and informal, and where helping may or may not be a part of other primary roles. Unlike in formal counselling and psychotherapy, helpers who use basic counselling skills are often already in dual relationships with clients: for example, supervisor–worker, speech therapist–patient or hotel manager–guest. Since it impossible to generalize for every helping context, this chapter focuses on helping contacts where psychological agendas predominate for clients. Should helpers talk about themselves at all when working with clients? How can helpers show genuineness and humanity if they stay as blank screens to clients? Helper self-disclosure relates to the ways in which they let themselves be known to clients.

Helper self-disclosure, even in brief helping contacts, can be for good or ill. Possible positive consequences of helpers talking about themselves include providing new insights and perspectives, demonstrating a useful skill, equalizing and humanizing the helping relationship, normalizing clients' difficulties, instilling hope and offering reassurance. There are, however, grave dangers in helpers inappropriately talking about themselves. For example, they may hijack the focus of the helping conversation to themselves and burden clients with their problems. Furthermore, they may come across as weak and unstable when vulnerable clients want helpers who have 'got their act together'.

Usually the term 'self-disclosure' refers to face-to-face intentional verbal disclosure. However, there are numerous other ways in which helpers disclose, including their vocal and body messages, their availability, office decor, phone, written or email communications and size of fees! A useful distinction exists between self-involving responses and self-disclosing responses. Another way of stating this is that there are at least two major dimensions of helper self-disclosure: showing involvement and disclosing personal information.

Showing involvement

There is a story about a psychoanalyst who would go down to the coffee shop, leaving her cassette-recorder on in the consulting room to listen to her patients' free associations and dreams. One day a patient, who was meant to be on the couch, came into the coffee shop and the following dialogue took place.

Psychoanalyst: What are you doing down here? You're meant to be in psychoanalysis.
Patient: Don't worry, doc. I've left my cassette-player on up there speaking into your cassette-recorder.

Unlike this caricature of a totally detached psychoanalyst, helpers can show involvement to assist the helping process. Disclosures that show involvement can humanize helping so that clients feel that they are relating to real people. There is a 'here-and-now' quality in showing involvement by sharing reactions to clients. Three areas for disclosing involvement are responding to specific client disclosures, responding to clients as people, and responding to clients' vulnerability. Box 14.1 provides examples of helper statements for each area.

Box 14.1 Examples of disclosures showing involvement

Responding to specific disclosures
I'm delighted.

That's great.

That's terrible.

I'm really sorry to hear that.

Responding to clients as people

I admire your courage.

I appreciate your honesty.

Responding to clients' vulnerability

I'm available if you get really low.

I'm very concerned about what you're going through.

Disclosing personal information

Disclosure of personal information may be either initiated by helpers or in response to clients' questions. One area of disclosing personal information relates to the helper's qualifications and experience. Sometimes this information is already available to clients, but if not, helpers need to decide what and how much to reveal. When helpers are asked about their qualifications and experience, there is much to be said for honest but brief answers.

Another area of revealing personal information relates to details of helper's private life and outside interests. Since helping settings range from the very informal to very formal, the appropriateness of degrees of disclosure about one's private life may differ greatly from one setting to another. For example, in peer helping, it can be part of the original contract that each party discusses problems in their private lives. In some informal settings, such as helping in youth centres, helpers may selectively reveal details of their private lives and interests as part of the relationship-building process with their clientele. For example, youth workers with interests in certain sporting activities, disco dancing and pop music, might well want to share these interests when conversing with groups of young people. However, when helping individual clients, disclosing such personal information might be much less appropriate. In instances where helping takes place in conjunction with many other primary roles, such as doctor, welfare officer or priest, helpers are less likely to disclose details of their private lives and interests.

Sometimes helpers' previous or present experiences in their personal and working lives are similar to those currently experienced by clients. Helpers who disclose personal information about similar experiences can help clients to feel that they understand what they are going through. For instance, unemployed people might feel differently about helpers who share that they too have been unemployed. Additionally, such disclosures can make it easier for clients to talk about their own experiences. Box 14.2 contains an example of the disclosure of personal information that strengthens the collaborative working relationship.

Box 14.2 Example of disclosing personal information

Helper: Brian, as you've been talking of your experiences of being unemployed, it reminds me of a period in my life when I was out of a job and really scared that I would never find another one. Though clearly our experiences differ, I think I do have some idea of what you're going through.

Brian: Thanks for that. One of the hardest things about being unemployed is feeling so bloody alone and useless. It's as if I'm burdening and boring people by talking about it.

In some types of helping, disclosure of shared experiences is a mandatory part of the process: for instance, striving for honesty in owning up to one's addiction is integral to Alcoholics Anonymous and some drug addiction programmes. Furthermore, in such programmes there are also testimonials by those who are no longer drinking or taking drugs. Such personal information disclosures provide evidence that, even though it may involve an agonizing struggle, people can be successful in containing their addictions.

Assuming they consider self-disclosure of personal information appropriate, helpers have many choices in how they do this. One choice is whether to restrict oneself to past experiences or discuss current experiences. Another choice is that of how honest to be or how much detail to share. A further choice is that of whether to go beyond disclosing facts to disclosing feelings: for instance, not only having been unemployed but then having to struggle against feelings of depression and uselessness. Additional helper choices include revealing how they coped with their experiences and how they feel about them now. In the kind of brief helping assumed by the Relating–Understanding–Changing helping process model, helpers will not have the opportunity to develop the 'relational depth' that counsellors and psychotherapists achieve with some clients later in a series of helping sessions.

Below are some guidelines for helpers concerning appropriate disclosure of personal information where helper experiences are similar to those of clients.

1   *Talk about oneself* In general, avoid disclosing the experience of third parties whom one either knows or has heard about.
2   *Talk about past experiences* A risk of disclosing current experiences, such as going through a divorce, is that helpers have insufficient emotional distance to ensure that their own agendas do not become intermingled with those of their clients.
3   *Be to the point* Helpers should avoid slowing down or defocusing the helping through lack of relevance or talking too much.
4   *Use good vocal and body messages* Helpers need to be genuine and consistent with their vocal and body messages matching their verbal disclosures.
5   *Be sensitive to clients' reactions* Helpers should possess sufficient awareness to realize when their disclosures might be helpful to clients and when they might be unwelcome or a burden.
6   *Be sensitive to helper–client differences* Expectations of helpers differ across cultures, social class, race and gender and so do expectations regarding appropriateness of helper self-disclosure.
7   *Share personal experiences sparingly* Helpers should be very careful not to switch the focus of helping from clients to themselves.
8   *Beware of countertransference* Countertransference refers to negative and positive feelings towards clients based on unresolved areas in helpers' own lives. Intentionally or unintentionally, some helpers disclosure personal information to manipulate clients to meet unfulfilled needs for approval, intimacy and sex. This possibility highlights the importance of helpers being aware of their motivation and behaving ethically.

ACTIVITIES

Activity 14.1 Showing involvement

1   With respect to your present or future helping work, write down the sorts of situations in which it might be appropriate for you to show involvement to clients early on in helping.
2   Using Box 14.1 on pages 94–5 as a guide, formulate one or more showing involvement disclosures in each of the following areas:
   • responding to specific client disclosures;
   • responding to clients as people; and
   • responding to clients' vulnerability.

3 Work with a partner and use basic counselling skills to help her/him to discuss a personal concern or to role-play a client. During the course of a mini session, try on a few occasions to make disclosures showing involvement. Afterwards, your partner gives you feedback on the impact of your showing involvement disclosures. Then reverse roles.

Activity 14.2 Disclosing personal information

1 With regard to your present or future helping work, write down the sorts of situations in which it might be appropriate for you to share personal information with clients early on in helping.
2 For each situation formulate one or more disclosing personal information response.
3 Work with a partner and use basic counselling skills to help her/him to discuss a personal concern or to role-play a client. During the course of a mini session, try on one or more appropriate occasion to disclose personal information. Afterwards, your partner gives you feedback on the impact of your personal information disclosures. Then reverse roles.

15 Managing resistances and making referrals

This chapter on managing resistances and making referrals concerns two areas that confront many helpers. Many helpers see clients who have been referred by others and have not come of their own free will. Furthermore, when helping starts, clients can still resist participating fully in collaborative working relationships. In addition, in some instances helpers may consider that they are not the right people to help clients and that others might do the job better. This raises the issue of whether and how to refer clients elsewhere.

Managing resistances

Resistances may be broadly defined as anything that gets in the way of helping. Resistances are clients' feelings, thoughts and communications that frustrate, impede, slow down and sometimes stop the helping process. Reluctance, which is unwillingness or disinclination on the part of potential or actual clients to enter into the helping process, is an aspect of being resistant about helping. Some clients do not see the need for help. They reluctantly see helpers to meet others' wishes: for instance, children sent by teachers or parents, or substance abusers and perpetrators of domestic violence sent by the courts. Many clients are ambivalent about discussing their problems with helpers. At the same time as wanting change, many may have anxieties about changing from their safe and known ways and also about the helping process: for instance, revealing personal information. Furthermore, clients may resist helpers whose very behaviour is too discrepant from their expectations and what from they think they need.

How to manage resistances

The following are some suggestions for understanding and dealing with resistances early on in helping. Many of these skills are also relevant for later sessions and contacts. Because there are so many variations and reasons for resistances within the broad range of contexts in which helpers use basic counselling skills, it is impossible to cover all contingencies.

Use active listening skills

Helpers may wrongly attribute the sources of clients' resistances by being too quick to blame them for lack of cooperation and progress. Beginning and even more experienced helpers may both sustain and create clients' resistances through poor listening skills. Resistances are a normal part of the early stages of helping. By using good active listening skills, helpers do much to build the trust needed to lower resistances. Some clients' resistances manifest themselves in aggression. Rather than helpers feeling the need to justify themselves and become sucked into competitive contests, one approach to handling such aggression is to reflect it back, locating the feelings clearly in the client but indicating that the anger has been picked up loud and clear. Where clients provide reasons for their hostility, helpers can reflect these too. Helpers, by just showing clients that they understand their internal frames of reference, especially if this is done consistently, can diminish resistances.

Join with clients

Sometimes helpers can lower clients' resistances by helping them feel that they have a friend at court. For instance, helpers can initially listen and offer support to children expressing resentment about parents.

Khalid:	I think coming here is a waste of time. My mum and dad keep picking on me and they are the ones who need help.
Family helper:	You feel angry about coming here because your parents are the people with problems.
Khalid:	Yeah (and then proceeds to share his side of the story).

In the above instance the helper accepted Khalid's focus on parental deficiencies and used his need to mention parental injustices to build the helping relationship. Were the client to continue to complain about his parents, after an appropriate period of time the helper might have built up enough trust and goodwill either for Khalid to focus on his own behaviour of his own accord or for the helper to assist him to make this switch.

Give permission to discuss reluctance and fears

If helpers receive overt or subtle messages from clients that they have reservations about seeing them, they can bring the agenda out into the open and give clients permission to elaborate. In the following example, a parole officer responds to a juvenile delinquent's seeming reluctance to disclose anything significant.

Parole officer: I detect you are unwilling to open up to me because I'm your parole officer. If I'm right, I'm wondering what specifically worries you about that?

Where appropriate, helpers can also give clients permission to discuss differences in helper–client characteristics, for instance culture and race, that can make it harder for some clients to participate in helping.

Invite cooperation

Establishing good collaborative working relationships with clients both prevents and also overcomes many resistances. Helpers can make statements early on in the helping process that can aim to create the idea of a partnership, a shared endeavour in which clients and helpers work together to assist clients to deal with their problems and thus to lead happier and more fulfilled lives.

Enlist client self-interest

Helpers can assist clients to identify reasons or gains for them of participating in helping. For instance, children who perceive their parents as picking on them and as the ones with problems can be assisted to see that they themselves might be happier if they develop better skills for coping with parents. Furthermore, questions that challenge clients with the adequacy of their own behaviour may enlist self-interest. Such questions include 'Where is your current behaviour getting you?' and 'How is that behaviour helping you?' Questions that encourage clients to think about goals are also useful: for example, 'What are your goals in the situation?' and 'Wouldn't you like to be more in control of your life?'

Reward silent clients for talking

Some clients find it difficult to talk whether or not they are with helpers. Others may find it particularly difficult to talk to helpers. Without coming on too strong, helpers can respond more frequently and more obviously. For example, helpers may use more small rewards when clients talk. In addition, helpers can offer encouragement by reflecting and making the most of what clients say. Furthermore, helpers can reflect the difficulty certain clients have in talking, even though they may not have verbalized this themselves.

Making referrals

Early on in helping and also later, helpers may face decisions about referring clients elsewhere. Even experienced counsellors have types of clients with whom they feel more competent and comfortable and others less so. Noted psychotherapist, Arnold Lazarus, states that an important helping principle is to 'Know your limitations and other clinicians' strengths'. Referrals should be made where other helpers have skills that an individual helper does not possess or have more appropriate personal styles for particular clients. Important ethical issues surround referral, especially where other helpers have more expertize with specific problems, for instance, with substance abuse or unwanted pregnancy.

Referral may not be an either/or matter. Sometimes helpers continue working with clients but also refer them to other helping professionals. Alternatively, helpers may be the recipients of referrals from other helping professionals who continue working with the same client. Sometimes helpers can refer clients to gain additional knowledge about their problems. For example, helpers should refer clients with concentration blocks or difficulty performing sexually for medical checks. Then, depending on the outcome of these checks, helpers have relevant information about whether or not to continue seeing them either alone, in conjunction with a physician or not at all.

On many occasions helpers can refer the clients' problem rather than the clients to other helping professionals. For example, helpers can discuss with colleagues or supervisors how best to assist certain clients. Occasions when helpers may refer clients' problems rather than the clients include: when they are the only helper available in an area; when clients state a clear preference for continuing working with them; and when clients are unlikely to follow through on referrals.

How to refer

The following are some considerations and skills for making referrals. Helpers can be too ready to refer clients and should avoid doing so unnecessarily. Sometimes it is better for clients to continue working with them. Under-confident helpers should tune in to their anxieties and fears about seeing certain clients. They can endeavour to build their confidence and skills to expand the range of clients with whom they can work. Wherever possible, helpers should ensure that they have adequate supervision and support.

As time goes by, helpers should try to develop a good feel for their strengths and limitations. They should be realistic about the kinds of clients with whom they work well and those with whom they are less skilled. Helpers also need to be realistic about their workloads and set appropriate limits on them.

Good referrals are more likely to be made to people whom helpers know and trust, rather than 'blind'. Helpers should get to know the relevant resources available in their locations so that they can avoid making referrals to helpers about whose competence they are unsure. In addition, even if they do know the other helpers, it may be wise to check if they have the time available for seeing new clients.

Where possible, helpers should make referrals early on. If they defer referrals longer than necessary, they waste clients' and their own time. Furthermore, it is preferable to refer clients before they emotionally bond with their helpers.

When making referrals, helpers should calmly explain to clients why this may be a good idea. They should be able to support explanations from information already revealed by clients. It is important that clients are absolutely clear about how to make contact with the other helpers. Helpers can hand out business cards or write down addresses and phone numbers.

Helpers should be prepared to spend time discussing any queries and emotional reactions clients may have to their referral suggestions. If the clients are in crisis, they may need to accompany them to the other helper's office. Another consideration is whether and what information they should provide for the next or a different helper. Helpers can discuss such issues with their clients and, if necessary, ask permission to share information.

Lastly, helpers should build their own support networks. Such support networks provide professional support when they want to refer clients' problems rather than the clients themselves. Helpers' support networks are likely to overlap with their referral networks, but some members' roles are different. For example, helpers can discuss clients' problems with supervisors and trainers, but they are less likely to refer clients to them.

ACTIVITIES

Activity 15.1 Managing resistances

1   For a helping setting in which you either work or might work, list the main ways clients may show resistances early on in helping.
2   Formulate the following kinds of managing resistances responses:
    • joining response;
    • permission to discuss reluctance and fears response; and
    • enlisting client self-interest response.

Activity 15.2 Making referrals

In regard to either your current or future helping work:

1   When might you refer clients to other helpers?
2   What categories of helpers do you require in your referral network?
3   What categories of helpers do you require in your support network – when you refer problems but not clients?
4   What are some considerations in making good referrals?
5   When might you be at risk of making unnecessary referrals?

16   Facilitating problem solving

Though a simplification, in Chaper 6 I mentioned that facilitating problem solving and improving communications/actions and thoughts are two approaches that helpers and clients can take when addressing issues of change. To some extent the two approaches overlap. In the facilitating problem solving approach, helpers stay close to clients' internal frames of reference and mainly draw upon clients' suggestions for change. In the improving communications/actions and thoughts approach, helpers are more active in working with clients to specify the behaviours requiring improvement and in helping them to achieve this end.

The facilitating problem solving approach, the focus of the present chapter, is not restricted to beginning helpers. Experienced helpers, too, need to be very skilled at combining active listening skills with probes designed to clarify goals, explore options for attaining them and develop plans to implement a chosen option.

Clarifying goals

When some clients, with the assistance of their helpers, have clarified their understanding of the key dimensions of their problems and problem situations, of their own accord they then clarify goals and proceed to attain them. Helpers use good active listening skills to facilitate these clients to tap into their own resources and act appropriately in problem situations. The main thrust of Carl Rogers' person-centred approach to counselling and helping is that helpers should provide the emotional climate and facilitative conditions so that clients can get in touch with what they truly feel as a basis for taking effective action in their lives. Helpers should be sensitive to the extent that clients just want them to be there as skilled listeners while they do their own work.

On other occasions, helpers can follow up summaries that pull together the main dimensions of problem situations with questions that assist clients to clarify their goals in dealing with them. When first meeting helpers, some clients are so overwhelmed that they lose sight of what they really want to achieve. As time goes by, many clients will have calmed down sufficiently so that they can think fairly rationally about their goals. However, these clients may still require assistance from helpers to articulate these goals.

Helpers might start assisting clients to address issues of change with a structuring statement along the lines of 'Now we have clarified and summarized many of the main dimensions of your problem situation, perhaps we can now try and clarify your goals in it. Do you think this would be helpful?' Many clients will answer 'yes' right away. Some might answer 'What do you mean?' If so, helpers can tactfully explain to clients that clarifying where they want to go makes it easier to decide how to get there.

Helpers can distinguish between outcome goals, 'Where do I want to go?', and process goals, 'What are my sub-goals or steps in getting where I want to go?' Here I focus on outcome goals. Often, when prac- tising as a counselling psychologist, I have found that clients start by being insufficiently creative when thinking about goals for specific sit- uations. Rather than latch on to the first goal that comes to mind, helpers can assist clients to generate and consider a range of goals by asking 'What are your options in setting goals?' Such goals can be both positive, 'What do I want to achieve?', and negative, 'What do I want to avoid?', and are often a mixture of the two. Box 16.1 lists some ques- tions that helpers can use to assist clients in clarifying their goals in problem situations.

Helpers should avoid bombarding clients with questions about goals. In most instances, small is beautiful. A few well-chosen questions that get to the heart of what clients want to achieve and avoid are all that is necessary. However, sometimes helpers may need to facilitate clients in exploring deeper goals and the values that underpin them rather than surface goals. In all instances, helpers should respect clients' rights to set their own goals and also intersperse active listening with their questions to clarify goals.

Box 16.1 Some questions for clarifying goals

What are your goals in the situation?

What would you consider a successful outcome?

What are your options in setting goals?

What do you want to achieve in the situation:

• for yourself;
• for one or more others; or
• for your relationship, if appropriate?

What do you want to avoid in the situation:

• for yourself;
• for one or more others; or
• for your relationship, if appropriate?

Generating and exploring options

Questions that clarify goals are about ends. Questions for generating and exploring options are about the means to achieve the clients' ends. Just as clients can latch on to the first goal that comes into mind, so they can latch on to the first method of achieving a goal that comes into their heads.

Box 16.2 is a case example that highlights the outcomes of using, generating and exploring options questions to assist clients to attain goals. Often, once clients set goals, they feel stuck and do not know how to proceed. Skilled questioning to help clients to generate and explore options assists them to put on their thinking caps and use their minds creatively. Many clients are wiser than they know, but have insufficient confidence and skills to get their wisdom out into the open.

Helpers may need to assist clients to think about the consequences of options. Often it is best to generate options first and assess consequences afterwards. Prematurely assessing the consequences of options can interfere with the creative process of generating them.

Questions and comments for generating and exploring options include: 'Given your goal of _____ [specify goal], what ways might you attain it?', 'Just let the ideas flow without editing them too much', 'Are there any other ways that you might approach the situation?' and 'What might be the consequences of doing that?' Notice that all of these questions and comments put the onus of coming up with ideas on the client. Helpers should resist the temptation to take over and own clients' problem situations.

Box 16.2 Generating options to attain goals: case example

The problem situation

Robbie, 15, enters helping worried about his deteriorating relationship with his dad. Robbie is disturbed about the aggressive way his dad sometimes relates to his mum. Robbie handles his difficulties with his dad by alternating aggression with withdrawal. Robbie admits his dad does a lot for him and might respond favourably to moves to improve the relationship. Robbie wants to get on better, but fears his own resentment will get in the way. Robbie feels lonely much of the time, partly because he is too wrapped up in what is going on at home. Robbie discusses his problem with Charlotte, who is a teacher with pastoral care duties at his school.

Robbie's goals

Goals that Robbie wants to achieve within the next month:

1   To develop a better relationship with my dad.
2   To have more friends in and out of school.

Robbie's options

With the assistance of Charlotte, the following are some of the options that Robbie generates to attain his goals.

Goal 1: Options for developing a better relationship with my dad:

• greeting dad in a friendly way in the morning and when he gets home from work;
• saying 'thank you' when dad does things for me;
• letting dad know more about what is going on in my life;
• telling dad how upset I get when he and mum row; and
• finding some things that dad and I can do together.

Goal 2: Options for having more friends in and out of school:

- complaining far less about home when I am at school;
- spending more time with the people I really like;
- being more open to accepting invitations;
- participating more in school activities; and
- spending more time with girls.

When working with clients, helpers should start by keeping matters simple. For instance, they might focus on exploring options to attain one goal and then only assist the client to generate a few options. If necessary, helpers should consider using either notepads or whiteboards. It is well nigh impossible for them and their clients to keep in their heads the kind of detail I have illustrated in the Robbie case example.

Assisting planning

Once clients have generated options, they need to choose those that they are prepared to implement. Plans can range from the simple to the detailed. Helper skills for facilitating planning include assisting clients to choose options for attaining their goals, encouraging them to be specific about how they can implement the options and, where appropriate, sequencing them into a step-by-step plan which has a time frame. When plans have been formulated, helpers can explore clients' commitments to implementing them, including how to deal with any anticipated difficulties and set-backs. Furthermore, helpers can encourage clients to write down plans to make them easier to remember. If clients are returning for subsequent sessions or helping contacts, helpers can assist them in monitoring progress and in adjusting plans, if necessary. Box 16.3 illustrates a plan that Robbie and his helper, Charlotte, formulate to meet his goal of developing a better relationship with his dad.

Sometimes helpers and clients either have, or think that they have, little time to develop plans. Take the example of a helper working with Amy, who after 15 years of marriage feels the pressing need to inform her husband Bruce that she feels cold and uninvolved in their relationship, even though she respects him and most of the time their relationship is friendly. For some time Amy has been building up to this discussion with Bruce and wants to hold it this evening. Her helper

---

> **Box 16.3 Example of a plan**
>
> **Robbie's goal**
> To develop a better relationship with my dad.
>
> **Robbie's plan**
> Step 1: Starting today, every day greet dad in a friendly way in the morning and when he gets back from work. Also, starting today, say 'thank you' when dad does things for me.
>
> Step 2: Starting seven days from now, share more about what is going on at school with dad at least twice a week.
>
> Step 3: Starting two weeks from now, engage in at least one joint pleasant activity with dad at least once a month.
>
> Step 4: When I am ready, tell dad how upset I get when he and mum row.

asks her 'What do you want to achieve?' Amy replies she wants to bring her feelings out in the open and see how Bruce responds. The helper then asks Amy 'What are skilful ways to handle the talk with Bruce?' and 'What are unskilful ways?' The helper encourages Amy to be more specific about how she intends to handle her discussion with Bruce this evening.

ACTIVITY

Activity 16.1 Facilitating problem solving

1 Work with a partner who presents either a problem situation of her/his own or one based on a client seen elsewhere.
2 Conduct a helping session in which the helper builds a collaborative working relationship with the client, together helper and client clarify the problem situation, and the session ends with a helper summary of the main ground covered so far.
3 Then helper and client adopt a facilitating problem solving approach to change including:

- clarifying goals;
- generating and exploring options for attaining goals;
- developing a plan; and
- exploring the client's commitment to and anticipating difficulties in implementing the plan.

4 After the session ends, hold a sharing and feedback discussion. It can be a good idea to videotape the session and play it back as part of the sharing and feedback.

5 If appropriate, reverse roles.

17   Coaching, demonstrating and rehearsing

When adopting the improving communications/actions and thoughts approach to change, helpers often find themselves in the position of using training skills to assist clients to behave differently. Three important training skills are client-centred coaching, demonstrating and rehearsing.

Client-centred coaching

When training clients in improving how they communicate, act and think, it is important that helpers allow them to retain ownership of their problems and problem situations. Furthermore, helpers should strive to maintain good collaborative working relationships. The urge to teach and instruct can override respect for clients' potentials to lead their own lives and make the decisions that work best for them.

A useful distinction is that between helper-centred coaching and client-centred coaching. Helper-centred coaching essentially takes the jug and mug approach: helpers are the jugs pouring knowledge and skills into clients' mugs. Helpers are in control and their comments take the form: 'First you do this, then you do that, then you do that . . .' and so on. Clients are passive receptacles who are allowed to assume little responsibility for the pace and direction of their learning. In reality, very few helpers would work as crudely as I have depicted.

Client-centred coaching respects clients as autonomous human beings. Helpers as client-centred coaches develop plans to attain goals in conjunction with clients and draw out and build upon clients' existing knowledge and skills. Furthermore, they allow clients to participate in decisions about the pace and direction of learning, and also assist them to improve their knowledge and skills in such ways that clients can help themselves after terminating helping.

Take the example of providing feedback about clients' performances when rehearsing how to improve their verbal, vocal and body messages in a specific situation. Helper-centred coaches provide the feedback themselves as though they are the experts. Client-centred coaches try to develop the expertise of clients by asking them to evaluate their own performances before providing feedback themselves. Even when they do provide feedback, client-centred coaches are prepared to discuss it and leave clients with the final say regarding its validity for them.

Demonstrating

Helpers can use demonstrations to assist clients to develop different and better ways of communicating/acting and thinking. Furthermore, helpers can demonstrate how to accompany communicating or acting differently with appropriate self-talk. The following are some ways that helpers can demonstrate improved ways of behaving.

- *Live* Probably most helping demonstrations are live. Helpers may use live demonstrations when initially presenting different ways of behaving and when coaching clients afterwards. Live demonstrations have the advantage of here-and-now spontaneity. In addition, helpers can interact with clients and modify their demonstrations as appropriate. Unless a recording is made, a limitation of live demonstration is that clients have no copy to watch or listen to on their own. Helpers can also encourage clients to observe live demonstrations in their everyday lives. For instance, shy people can be encouraged to observe and learn from the social skills of those more outgoing.
- *Recorded* Especially if helpers are working with client populations who have similar problems, they can record their own videotape or audio cassette demonstrations. When making recordings, helpers can erase and correct poor efforts until they get it right. In addition, they can use recordings made by other people, some of which are professionally made: for instance, relaxation cassettes. Advantages of audio cassette and videotape demonstrations are that they can be loaned to clients and be listened to or viewed repeatedly.

- *Written* Written demonstrations are more appropriate for helping clients to change how they think than to change how they communicate and act. However, written demonstrations that contain visual images, such as cartoon characters, can convey desirable communications and actions.
- *Visualized* Helpers can ask clients to visualize or imagine the demonstration scenes that they describe. Clients can be asked to visualize either themselves or someone else performing the targeted communications or actions. Visualized demonstrations are only appropriate for clients who can imagine scenes adequately. A potential drawback is that, even when instructions are given well, there may be important differences between what helpers describe and what clients imagine. In general clients visualize best when relaxed.

Demonstrator skills

Helpers must know their material thoroughly to demonstrate competently. For example, if helpers have a sound grasp of assertion skills, they are more likely to demonstrate these skills adequately than if less sure of their ground. Helpers need to pay attention to characteristics of the demonstration. One issue is whether to demonstrate incorrect as well as correct behaviours. Helpers may plan briefly to demonstrate negative behaviours as a way of highlighting positive ones. However, helpers should make sure not to confuse clients and always have the major emphasis on correct rather than incorrect behaviours.

Helpers should take care how they introduce demonstrations. They may increase clients' attention by telling them what to look out for and also informing them that afterwards they will be asked to perform what has been demonstrated. During and at the end of demonstrations helpers may ask clients whether they understand the points shown. Furthermore, clients can summarize the main points of demonstrations. Probably the best way for helpers to check clients' learning is to observe and coach them as they perform demonstrated communications/actions and thoughts.

Rehearsing

Rehearsing is a possibly less threatening expression than role-playing. Some clients become uncomfortable at the idea of role-playing. Feeling shy and vulnerable already, they think they will further expose themselves in role-plays. Helpers may need to explain to clients that rehearsing can help them by allowing them to try out communicating differently in an environment where mistakes do not really matter. Doing this can provide knowledge and confidence for communicating effectively in actual problem situations.

One way to start rehearsing is for helpers to demonstrate targeted communications with or without the client playing the other person. For example, in Box 17.1, the helper Ian demonstrates Liz's communication goals, with Liz role-playing a friend who is asking her to stop studying and go out, before inviting Liz to role-play herself while Ian plays the part of the friend. Ian then coaches Liz through a number of rehearsals where she assertively responds to her friend's request to go out.

Box 17.1 Example of demonstrating, rehearsing and coaching

Liz, 23, a social work student who has got behind in her work and is now coming up to her final examinations, is seeing a helper, Ian. One of Liz's problems is that she finds it very hard to say no to her friends who call by her room in the evening and ask her to go out with them. More often than not, Liz gives in and joins them at the expense of her work. In conjunction with Ian, Liz develops the following assertive verbal response to a request to go out: 'I appreciate your coming round, but my final exams are in three weeks and I'm way behind in my revision. Until my exams are over, I can only go out on Saturday evenings. I hope that you will understand.' With Ian's help, Liz decides that her vocal messages should be calm and firm. Regarding her body messages, Liz wants to make good eye contact and keep a pleasant facial expression.

Ian then asks Liz to role-play a friend coming round to her room to ask her out and says he will be Liz. Liz, role-playing her friend, asks Ian about joining them to go out. Ian responds demonstrating the targeted verbal, vocal and body messages upon which they previously agreed. Ian asks Liz how she experiences this response. Liz is happy with the response so they reverse roles and Ian, as the friend, asks the going-out question. Liz's response is insufficiently assertive. After asking Liz to evaluate herself, Ian coaches Liz, including demonstrating how he observed Liz's verbal, vocal and body messages. With continued coaching by Ian, Liz then tries her response a few more times until she feels reasonably confident that, if asked the going-out question by a friend, she can perform competently.

Helpers and clients may need to generate and rehearse alternative scripts. Helpers should train diversely rather than rigidly in order to provide clients with the flexibility to communicate well across a range of contingencies. Helpers can facilitate clients' contributions to the discussion prior to making their own suggestions. For instance, Ian could ask Liz 'What do you think are the main ways in which your friends or friends might respond to your assertive statement about not going out with them?' Then for each of the main ways identified, Ian could ask 'What verbal, vocal and bodily messages do you need to use to respond effectively?' Then, Liz and Ian could rehearse effective communications for different ways the friend or friends might respond.

Helpers and clients need to process each rehearsal. Helpers can ask clients questions like: 'How do you think you did?', 'How were you feeling in that rehearsal?' and 'What difficulties might you face in communicating like that in the real situation?' In addition, helpers can provide both feedback and encouragement. Sometimes, helpers can audio record or video record rehearsals and use the playback for feedback and discussion.

ACTIVITIES

Activity 17.1 Using demonstrating skills

Work with a partner, with one taking the role of helper and the other taking the role of client. Client and helper hold a discussion to choose a specific communication that the client wants to improve. Do not attempt too much. The helper then goes through the following steps in a demonstration:

- cueing the client what to observe;
- demonstrating each of the verbal, vocal and body message components of the communication and then putting all three together (your partner may role-play the other person as you demonstrate); then
- asking the client to summarize the main points of the demonstration.

Afterwards hold a sharing and discussion session focused on the helper's use of demonstration skills. If necessary repeat the demonstration until the helper feels she/he has obtained some degree of competence in using demonstration skills.

Then reverse roles.

Activity 17.2 Using rehearsing and coaching skills

Work with a partner, with one taking the role of helper and the other taking the role of client. Either for a specific communication that was demonstrated in Activity 17.1 or for another specific communication that the client wants to improve, go through the following sequence:

- cueing the client what to observe;
- demonstrating each of the verbal, vocal and body message components of the communication and then putting all three together (your partner may role-play the other person as you demonstrate);
- asking the client to summarize the main points of the demonstration;
- introducing the idea of rehearsing the communication to your client;
- rehearsing and coaching your client to the point where, within the limits of this activity, she/he feels competent to perform the communication in real life competently. You may use audio cassette or videotape playback as part of the rehearsing and coaching process.

Afterwards, hold a sharing and discussion session focused on the helper's use of rehearsing and coaching skills. If necessary, allow the helper to rehearse and coach some more until the helper feels she/he has obtained some degree of competence in using rehearsing and coaching skills.

Then reverse roles.

18   Training clients in relaxation

Helpers can train clients in muscular and mental relaxation skills. Clients may use relaxation skills both for managing feelings like anger and anxiety and for dealing with problems such as tension headaches, hypertension and insomnia. Relaxation skills may be used alone or as part of more complex procedures such as systematic desensitization, a helping strategy described in my book *Essential Counselling and Therapy Skills* (see annotated bibliography).

Progressive muscular relaxation

The physical setting where helpers train should be conducive to relaxation. This involves absence of disruptive noise, interior decoration that is restful and lighting which may be dimmed. Clients may be taught to relax in recliner chairs, or on mattresses or, at the very least, in comfortable upright chairs with headrests.

From the start helpers can teach relaxation training as a useful skill for daily life. Furthermore, clients should understand that success at learning relaxation, just like success at learning any other skill, requires practice and that relaxation homework will be required. Before starting relaxation, helpers can suggest that clients wear loose-fitting, comfortable clothing both during interviews and when doing relaxation homework. Furthermore, that it is helpful to remove items such as glasses and shoes.

In training muscular relaxation there is a succession of instructions for each muscle group. Helpers can demonstrate how clients should go through a five-step tension-relax cycle for each muscle group. These steps are:

1   *Focus* – focus attention on a particular muscle group.
2   *Tense* – tense the muscle group.
3   *Hold* – maintain the tension for five to seven seconds.
4   *Release* – release the tension in the muscle group.
5   *Relax* – spend 20 to 30 seconds focusing on letting go of tension and further relaxing the muscle groups.

Clients need to learn this *focus–tense–hold–release–relax* cycle so that they may apply it in their homework.

Having explained the basic tension-relax cycle, helpers may then demonstrate it by going through the cycle in relation to their own right hand and forearm and at each stage asking their clients to do the same. Thus, 'I'm focusing all my attention on my right hand and forearm and I'd like you to do the same' progresses to 'I'm clenching my right fist and tensing the muscles in my lower arm . . .', then on to 'I'm holding my right fist clenched and keeping the muscles in my lower arm tensed . . .', followed by 'I'm now releasing as quickly as I can the tension from my right fist and lower arm . . .', ending with 'I'm relaxing my right hand and forearm, letting the tension go further and further and letting these muscles become more and more relaxed . . .'. The final relaxation phase tends to last from 30 to 60 seconds, frequently accompanied by helper relaxation 'patter' about letting the tension go and acknowledging and experiencing feelings of deeper and deeper relaxation as they occur. Having been through the tension-relax cycle once, especially in the initial sessions, the client may be instructed to go through it again, thus tensing and relaxing each muscle grouping twice.

Helpers are then likely to take clients through the muscle groups, demonstrating them as necessary. Box 18.1 shows 16 muscle groups and suggested tensing instructions. The arms tend to come at the beginning, since they are easy to demonstrate. For most clients, relaxing parts of the face is particularly important because the most marked anxiety-inhibiting effects are usually obtained there.

Once clients have learned how to tense the various muscle groups, they are instructed to keep their eyes closed during relaxation training and practice. Towards the end of relaxation sessions, helpers may ask clients for a summary of their relaxation, along the lines of 'Well, how was your relaxation today?' and discuss any issues that arise. Terminating relaxation sessions may be achieved by helpers counting from five to one and when they get to one asking their clients to wake up pleasantly relaxed as though from a peaceful sleep.

Box 18.1 Relaxation training muscle groups and tensing instructions

Muscle group	Tensing instructions*
Right hand and forearm	Clench your right fist and tense the muscles in your lower arm.
Right biceps	Bend your right arm at the elbow and flex your biceps by tensing the muscles of your upper right arm.
Left hand and forearm	Clench your left fist and tense the muscles in your lower arm.
Left biceps	Bend your left arm at the elbow and flex your biceps by tensing the muscles of your upper left arm.
Forehead	Lift your eyebrows as high as possible.
Eyes, nose and upper cheeks	Squeeze your eyes tightly shut and wrinkle your nose.
Jaw and lower cheeks	Clench your teeth and pull the corners of your mouth firmly back.
Neck and throat	Pull your chin down hard towards your chest yet resist having it touch your chest.
Chest and shoulders	Pull your shoulder blades together and take a deep breath.
Stomach	Tighten the muscles in your stomach as though someone was about to hit you there.
Right thigh	Tense the muscles of the right upper leg by pressing the upper muscle down and the lower muscles up.

Right calf	Stretch your right leg and pull your toes towards your head.
Right foot	Point and curl the toes of your right foot and turn it inwards.
Left thigh	Tense the muscles of the left upper leg by pressing the upper muscle down and the lower muscles up.
Left calf	Stretch your left leg and pull your toes towards your head.
Left foot	Point and curl the toes of your left foot and turn it inwards.

* With left-handed people, tensing instructions for the left side of the body should come before those for the right.

The importance of practising muscular relaxation may be further stressed at the end of the initial relaxation session. Clients are likely to be given the homework assignment of practising muscular relaxation for one or two 15-minute periods a day. Helpers should ask clients whether they anticipate any obstacles to practising, such as finding a quiet place, and help them to devise strategies for ensuring good homework. Helpers can also either make up cassettes of relaxation instructions that clients can take away for homework purposes or recommend existing relaxation training cassettes. There is some evidence that clients who record details of their relaxation practice are much more likely to continue doing it. Consequently, it may be helpful for helpers to give clients logs for monitoring their relaxation homework.

Brief muscular relaxation

Brief muscular relaxation skills aim to induce deep relaxation with less time and effort than the 16 muscle group relaxation procedure. When clients are proficient in full progressive muscular relaxation, helpers can introduce such skills. Brief relaxation skills are useful both in helping sessions and in daily life. The following are two examples.

Sequential brief relaxation

Here helpers can first instruct clients and then get them to give themselves the following instructions focused on tensing and relaxing in turn four composite muscle groupings.

> I'm going to count to ten in units of two. After each unit of two I will instruct you to tense and relax a muscle grouping. One, two . . . focus on your leg and feet muscles . . . tense and hold the tension in these muscles for five seconds . . . release . . . relax and enjoy the sensations of the tension flowing from your legs and feet. Three, four . . . take a deep breath and focus on your chest, shoulder and stomach muscles . . . tense and hold the tension in these muscles for five seconds . . . release . . . relax and enjoy the sensations of the tension flowing from your chest, shoulders and stomach. Five, six . . . focus on your face, neck and head muscles . . . tense and hold the tension in these muscles for five seconds . . . release . . . relax and enjoy the sensations of the tension flowing from your face, neck and head. Seven, eight . . . focus on your arm and hand muscles . . . tense and hold the tension in these muscles for five seconds . . . release . . . relax and enjoy the sensations of the tension flowing from your arms and hands. Nine, ten . . . focus on all the muscles in your body . . . tense all the muscles in your body together and hold for five seconds . . . release . . . relax and enjoy the sensations of the tension leaving your whole body as your relaxation gets deeper and deeper . . . deeper and deeper . . . deeper and deeper.

Simultaneous brief relaxation

As at the end of the previous example, helpers can instruct clients to tense all muscle groupings simultaneously. They can say:

> When I give the signal, I would like you to close your eyes very tightly, take a deep breath and simultaneously tense your arm muscles, your face, neck and throat muscles, your chest shoulder and stomach muscles, and your leg and foot muscles. Now take a deep breath and tense all your muscles . . . hold for five seconds . . . now release and relax as quickly and deeply as you can.

Mental relaxation

Helpers can assist clients to identify one or more favourite scenes conducive to feeling relaxed. Often clients visualize such restful scenes at the end of progressive muscular relaxation. The following is an example of a helper instructing a client to mentally relax.

> You're lying on an empty beach on a pleasant, sunny day, enjoying the sensations of warmth on your body. There is a gentle breeze. You can hear the peaceful noise of the sea steadily lapping against the nearby shore. You haven't a care in the world, and your enjoy your feelings of peace and calm, peace and calm, peace and calm and your feelings of relaxation and wellbeing.

Clients can visualize mental relaxation scenes independent of muscular relaxation. In addition, clients can use the 'counting to ten in groups of two' as a mental relaxation rather than as a muscular relaxation procedure. For example: 'One, two . . . focus on your leg and feet muscles . . . relax and enjoy the sensations of the tension flowing from your legs and feet.' As a mental relaxation procedure, clients edit out the tense, hold and release instructions.

Using coaching, demonstrating and rehearsing, helpers can train clients to develop mental relaxation procedures as self-helping skills. Clients may wish to record their self-instructions for playback outside of helping sessions.

Relaxation training considerations

Helpers differ in the number of sessions they use for relaxation training. Furthermore, clients differ in the speed with which they attain a capacity to relax. The late Dr Joseph Wolpe, a noted pioneer of behaviour therapy, taught progressive muscular relaxation in about six lessons and asked his patients to practice at home for two 15-minute sessions per day. He considered that it was crucial for clients to realize that the aim of relaxation training was not muscle control *per se*, but emotional calmness. Helpers may vary their relaxation training timetable according to their clients' needs and their own workload. Nevertheless, it is important that clients have sufficient sessions to learn relaxation adequately. Furthermore, clients need to practice their relaxation skills diligently and review progress with their helpers. In addition, it benefits many clients to integrate using relaxation skills into their daily lives.

ACTIVITY

Activity 18.1 Training a client in relaxation

Conduct a helping session in which partner A's task is to train partner B who acts as client in progressive muscular relaxation skills. During the session partner A:

- offers reasons for using progressive muscular relaxation;
- provides a live demonstration of tensing and relaxing the first muscle grouping in Box 18.1;
- makes up a progressive muscular relaxation cassette as she/he relaxes partner B using the five step tension-relax cycle;
- presents a mental relaxation scene at the end of the muscular relaxation;
- checks how relaxed the client became and provides further relaxation instructions for any muscle group where she/he still feels tense; and
- negotiates a progressive muscular relaxation homework practice assignment with the client.

Afterwards, both partners hold a sharing and discussion session and, if feasible, reverse roles.

19 Improving clients' self-talk

The next three chapters focus on working with how clients think. I present the three central mind skills of creating self-talk, rules and perceptions in an introductory way to provide a basic toolkit for helpers to assist clients in improving their thinking. Each of the chosen mind skills has wide applicability.

Helpers should proceed with great caution when assisting clients to alter specific thoughts. I have witnessed a number of beginning helpers jump in with faulty analyses of thinking which clients have not had the knowledge or confidence to challenge. In addition, helpers may not understand the mind skills properly themselves and therefore present them in a confused ways to clients. Furthermore, sometimes helpers rush through learning sequences rather than train clients in them thoroughly.

Herewith a few suggestions for working to improve how clients think. Helpers with some skills at working with their own thinking will probably have more insight into how to work with clients' thinking than those with poor mind skills. A good way for helpers to learn about how to use mind skills is to become proficient at using them in their own lives.

At first, it is probably easiest to focus on becoming proficient at working with one mind skill before broadening one's repertoire. Creating self-talk is a good mind skills area with which to start. One reason for this is that clients can create self-talk that supports any changed communication or action they target. Another reason is that virtually all helpers and clients are aware that they talk to themselves anyway. So requesting clients to do so in a more disciplined way is unlikely to be too strange for them.

Helpers can use visual aids when working with clients' thinking. I find using a whiteboard to be very helpful, especially when it comes to collaborating with clients to generate and refine more effective thoughts. I have seen some prominent psychotherapists use notepads. At an appropriate moment, helpers should encourage clients to make their own visual records by writing their improved thoughts down.

Helpers should remember that clients have usually built up and sustained their ways of faulty thinking over many years and, consequently, quick fixes are unlikely to succeed. They can protect clients if they keep offering good collaborative working relationships. In addition to using good active listening skills, helpers can coach clients in improving their thinking in client-centred rather than helper-centred ways. Helper humility is in order and, at all costs, beginning helpers should avoid being instant and overbearing experts.

Improving self-talk

I encourage readers to try the simple mind experiment of closing their eyes for 30 seconds and trying to think of nothing. Most readers will become very aware that they cannot rid themselves of self-talk.

Negative self-talk

My view is that people who talk to themselves are not crazy. It is what they choose to keep telling themselves that determines sanity or insanity. Here self-talk refers to how people talk to themselves before, during and after difficult situations. Often clients use negative self-talk that has the effect of creating or worsening self-defeating feelings, physical reactions and actions. Characteristics of negative self-talk include self-disparagement, stating that matters may get either worse or out of control, and focusing on past setbacks. Box 19.1 provides an illustration of a client who interferes with her effectiveness by using negative self-talk.

Coping self-talk

Coping self-talk contrasts with negative self-talk. Whereas negative self-talk impedes clients communicating and acting appropriately, coping self-talk enhances the likelihood of their performing well. Coping self-talk can be contrasted with mastery self-talk. Coping self-talk is about clients doing as well as they reasonably can rather than seeking the unrealistically high standards of mastery or perfection. The following are three key dimensions of coping self-talk.

Box 19.1 Example of negative self-talk

Val, 56, works for a local council and she gets very anxious about speaking in public. Three years ago, Val had a heart operation. Then, two years ago Val had to hand over the rostrum when her mind went blank. The time in which Val experiences most anxiety is the 30 to 60 seconds before she is due to speak, whether it be a formal speech or waiting for her turn to contribute at committee meetings. During this period, Val's self-talk consists of statements like 'Don't be so stupid', 'My anxiety may get out of control like two years ago' and 'I may have a heart attack'. Apart from the occasion two years ago when she could not continue, Val speaks in public very competently – nobody would know how anxious she feels.

Calming self-talk

Creating calming self-talk can assist clients to deal with problem situations in many ways. Before, during and after specific situations, they can calm their minds so that they can better handle unwanted feelings such as harmful anxiety or excessive anger. In addition, clients may wish to calm and relax their minds as a way of managing extraneous stresses that then impact on how they handle problem situations. A third purpose for creating calming self-talk is for clients to become more centred and focused when they wish to think through or talk through how best to communicate or act in problem situations. Clients' use of calming self-talk helps them to clear a psychological space for getting in touch with their feelings and thinking more sharply and deeply.

When introducing calming self-talk to clients, I may talk about the concept and then provide an example of a calming self-instruction like 'Relax'. Then I encourage clients to come up with some calming self-instructions of their own. Following that we may discuss which calming self-instructions the client prefers to use. In addition, I tell, demonstrate and coach clients in how to use a calm and measured voice when giving calming self-instructions. Sometimes, I highlight the difference by saying a phrase like 'Calm down' in a hurried and self-pressurizing way.

Cooling self-talk statements might be regarded as a sub-category of calming self-talk. Helpers can train clients who are prone to angry outbursts in cooling self-talk statements. Box 19.2 provides examples of both calming and cooling self-talk statements.

Box 19.2 Examples of calming and cooling self-talk statements

Calming self-talk statements
'Keep calm.'

'Slow down.'

'Relax.'

'Take it easy.'

'Take a deep breath.'

'Breathe slowly and regularly.'

'I can manage.'

Cooling self talk statements
'Cool it.'

'Count to ten.'

'Be careful.'

'Don't overreact.'

'Don't let my pride get in the way.'

'I can choose not to let myself get hooked.'

'Problem solve.'

Coaching self-talk

Coaching self-talk is no substitute for possessing the communication skills for achieving a task. The first step in coaching self-talk is to assist clients to break tasks down. Helpers can work with clients to think through systematic approaches to attaining goals in problem situations, including how to handle setbacks. Once plans are clear, clients require the ability to instruct themselves through the steps of implementing them.

Helpers need to emphasize self-talk about vocal and body as well as verbal messages. Take the example of Liz, the nursing student in Box 17.1 on page 115, who together with her helper Ian developed the assertive verbal message 'I appreciate your coming around, but my final exams are in three weeks and I'm way behind in my revision. Until my final exams are over, I can only go out on Saturday evenings. I hope that you will understand.' As well as coaching Liz in how to handle the face-to-face interaction, Ian could train Liz to rehearse in her mind giving herself appropriate self-instructions about her verbal, vocal and body messages. Liz's targeted vocal messages were to be calm and firm and her targeted body messages were to make good eye contact and to keep a pleasant facial expression. When on her own, Liz could then use visualized rehearsal to coach herself in coping better in the situation. Helpers can also assist clients to develop coaching self-talk statements to handle the different ways other people in problem situations might respond.

Affirming self-talk

I prefer the notion of affirming self-talk to that of positive self-talk. The danger of positive self-talk is that clients may tell themselves false positives that set them up for disappointment and failure. Affirming self-talk focuses on clients reminding themselves of realistic factors that count in their favour. Following are some aspects of affirming self-talk.

First, clients can tell themselves that they can cope. Sample self-statements include: 'I can handle this situation', 'My anxiety is a signal for me to use my coping skills' and 'All I have to do is to cope'. In addition, once clients cope with situations better, they can acknowledge this: for example, 'I used my coping skills and they worked.'

Second, clients can acknowledge their strengths. Often when clients are anxious about difficult situations, they forget their strengths. For example, when asking for dates, clients may genuinely possess good points, so they do not have to boast about them. Also, they may have good conversational skills that they can acknowledge and use rather than thinking about what may go wrong. In addition, clients can think about any successful experiences they may have had in the past in situations similar to the one they face.

Third, clients may become more confident if they acknowledge supportive people to whom they have access. For instance, relatives, friends, spouses and helping service professionals might each be sources of support, though not necessarily so. Just realizing that they have supportive people to whom they can turn may be sufficient to help some clients cope better with problem situations.

Putting it all together

Often calming, coaching and affirming self-talk statements are combined together. Box 19.3 continues the example of speech anxious Val from Box 19.1 to show how her helper assisted her to have the option of telling herself a composite calming, coaching and affirming coping self-talk statement. At the end of the session, Val writes down her coping self-talk statements for remembering, rehearsing and using outside of helping.

Box 19.3 Example of coping self-talk

Val's helper first put the word 'calming' on the whiteboard and then helped Val to identify statements she would find useful to calm herself down in the 30 to 60 seconds before speaking in public. The helper and Val repeated this process for coaching, affirming and composite statements. They ended with the following categories and statements written on the whiteboard.

Calming

Calm down.

It's not the end of the world.

Coaching

Rehearse my opening ideas and remarks.

No last minute changes.

My anxiety is a signal for me to use my coping skills.

I can retrieve mistakes.

Affirming

I've done this very well many times before.

Composite

Calm down. Rehearse my opening ideas and remarks. I've done this very well many times before.

ACTIVITY

Activity 19.1 Assisting a client to use coping self-talk

Work with a partner who either uses a personal concern or role-plays a client with a goal of using coping self-talk to manage a problem situation better. Within the context of a good collaborative working relationship and possibly using a whiteboard during the process:

- use speaking skills to describe the difference between negative and coping self-talk;
- use demonstrating skills;
- assist the client to identify any current negative self-talk;
- use coaching skills to help the client formulate calming, coaching, affirming and composite self-talk statements; and
- use negotiating homework skills.

Afterwards discuss and reverse roles. Playing back audio recordings or video recordings of rehearsal and practice sessions may assist learning.

20 Improving clients' rules

Helpers can assist clients to replace their demanding rules with ones that are more realistic. All people possess rule books that provide them with ready-made guidelines for leading their lives so that they do not need to think through all emerging situations from scratch. Most of the rules of well-functioning people are rational, realistic and based on their preferences for themselves, others and the environment. However, many clients seen by helpers contribute to disturbing themselves and making themselves unhappy because, often unawares, they possess some significant rigid or demanding rules, based on making irrational and unrealistic demands on themselves, others and the environment.

Detecting demanding rules

Unrealistic and demanding rules significantly contribute to many clients having difficulty managing their problems and problem situations. Demanding rules can lay the foundation for creating negative self-talk and inaccurate perceptions. For example, demanding rules like 'I must get approval' and 'I must be perfect' probably underlie many people's feelings of lack of confidence and wellbeing before starting new tasks, like writing essays. People can rationally prefer that readers like their essays and that they are competently written. These preferences are very different from essay writers who demand approval from readers and perfection from themselves.

Usually demanding rules contain realistic as well as unrealistic parts. For example, it is realistic for essay writers to want to write competently, but unrealistic to strive for perfection. Consequently, when assisting clients to alter a rule, helpers should focus on discarding the 20 to 30 per cent of the rule that is irrational rather than getting rid of it altogether.

The following are some indicators or signals for helpers to look out for when trying to detect demanding rules. They can pay attention to signs of inappropriate language. For example, demanding rules tend to be characterized by 'musts', 'oughts', 'shoulds' and 'have to's'. The following are four of the main demanding or, to use Albert Ellis's term, 'mustabatory' rules:

- 'I must be liked by everyone.'
- 'I must be perfectly competent.'
- 'Other people must do what I want.'
- 'Life must be fair.'

Persistent inappropriate feelings can signal that clients possess a demanding rule. The dividing line between appropriate and inappropriate feelings is not always clear. Life can be difficult, so appropriate feelings cannot simply be equated with 'positive' feelings like happiness, joy and accomplishment. Some 'negative' feelings like sadness, grief, fear and anger can be entirely appropriate for the contexts in which they occur. Helpers have to ask themselves questions like: 'Is this feeling appropriate for the situation?' and 'Is keeping feeling this way helping or harming the client?' Physical reactions may also signal demanding rules: for instance, persistent muscular tension could signal clients putting pressure on themselves for perfection or universal approval.

Inappropriate feelings, physical reactions and communications/actions are interrelated. If clients feel excessively angry because of a demanding rule, their physical level of arousal can impair their judgement to the point where they act violently and worsen rather than help their position. Relevant questions for helpers to ask themselves, and possibly clients too, include: 'Are clients' communications or actions helping or harming themselves or others?', 'Are they overreacting?' and 'Is their behaviour self-defeating?'

Box 20.1 provides an illustration of the consequences of stressed-out middle manager Pat's demanding rule 'I must devote all my energies to my job'. I have presented this example in the STC (Situation–Thoughts–Consequences) format that I first introduced in Chapter 12 when reviewing monitoring. Since this example has a second part in Box 20.3, I have indicated Pat's present thoughts and their consequences by putting (1) after T and C.

> **Box 20.1 Example of a demanding rule and its consequences**
>
> S   Workaholic middle manager Pat reaches her/his 40th birth-
>   day and becomes highly anxious.
>
> T(1) *Demanding rule*
>
>   'I must devote all my energies to my job.'
>
> C(1) *Negative feelings consequences* include anxiety, feeling very
>   stressed, irritability and low self-esteem.
>
>   *Negative physical reaction consequences* include mental exhaus-
>   tion, brownouts or memory losses due to exhaustion,
>   hypertension, migraine headaches and lower back pain.
>
>   *Negative communication/action consequences* include spending
>   excessive time at work – not always very productively –
>   neglecting her/his home life, and taking inadequate recreation.

How can helpers assist clients to create preferential rules to replace their demanding rules? Reading the signals, they can assist clients to identify what might be one or more underlying demanding rule(s) relevant to their problem situations. Then helpers can encourage clients to dispute, question and challenge their demanding rules and to restate them as preferential rules.

Disputing demanding rules

Albert Ellis considers disputing to be the most typical and often-used method of his Rational Emotive Behaviour Therapy. Disputing means challenging demanding rules. The main skill in challenging is that of scientific questioning. Helpers and clients can use reason, logic and facts to support, discard or amend any rule they consider to be potentially demanding. Box 20.2 shows two methods of disputing demanding rules.

Box 20.2 Two methods of disputing demanding rules

Functional disputing

Functional disputing aims to point out to clients that their rules may be interfering with attaining their goals. Typical questions are:

- 'Is it helping you?'
- 'How is continuing to think this way (or behave, or feel this way) affecting your life?'

Empirical disputing

Empirical disputing aims to help clients evaluate the factual components of their rules. Typical questions are:

- 'Where is the evidence that you must succeed at all important tasks you prefer?'
- 'Where is the proof that it is accurate?'
- 'Where is it written?'

When collaborating with clients to dispute their demanding rules, helpers are encouraged to elicit some questions from them: for instance, 'How might you question or challenge that rule?' When beginning helpers ask questions themselves, they should do so gently rather than forcefully and respond to clients' answers the same way. Furthermore, helpers can show restraint in the amount of questions they ask and remember to integrate active listening into the questioning and challenging process.

Stating preferential rules

Assisting clients to dispute their demanding rules should have the effect of loosening their effect on them. An added way of reducing the hold of demanding rules is to assist clients to restate them succinctly into preferential rules. Their challenges can be too many and varied to remember easily. Helpers can assist clients to create replacement statements that are easy to remember and recall. Sometimes, when time is very limited, helpers may eliminate time spent on questioning and challenging and move straight into helping clients restate a demanding rule as a preferential rule.

Helpers and clients can alter characteristics of demanding rules to become characteristics of preferential rules. An example is 'I'd *prefer* to do very well but I don't *have to.*' Clients can replace rules about mastery and perfection with rules incorporating competence, coping and 'doing as well as I can under the circumstances'. Furthermore, helpers can assist clients to refrain from rating their whole selves rather than evaluating how useful are their specific communications and actions.

In addition, helpers can assist clients to avoid making out that the world is absolutely awful by accepting that the world is imperfect and by refraining from exaggerating negative factors and possibilities. Helpers can also assist clients to eliminate an 'I can't stand it' attitude by encouraging them to tell themselves that they can stand the anxiety and discomfort arising from themselves, others and the environment not being as they would prefer them to be. Indeed, even in genuinely adverse circumstances, they may have many strengths on which they can rely and supportive persons to whom they can turn.

When working on restating rules, helpers should encourage clients to participate in the process by sharing their ideas. Some helpers use a whiteboard and work together with clients to get the wording just right for them to recall and use in future. The following are examples of how to restate four common demanding rules into preferential rules.

Demanding rule: I must be liked by everyone.
Preferential rule: I would prefer to have most people like me, but what is really important is that some significant people whom I respect like me and that I approve of myself.

Demanding rule: I must be perfectly competent.
Preferential rule: I prefer to strive towards high standards, but all I can do is the best I can.

Demanding rule: Other people must do what I want.
Preferential rule: I would prefer that others take my wishes into account, but I need to be sensitive to their wishes too.

Demanding rule: Life must be fair.
Preferential rule: I would prefer that life be fair, but the world is imperfect and I accept that there may be some aspects of it I cannot change.

Helpers need to encourage clients to work and practice hard to maintain their preferential rules. One approach is for helpers and clients to make cassettes of clients' initial demanding rules, their challenges and their restatements. Clients can also post in prominent positions reminder cards stating their preferential rules. In addition, clients can use visualized rehearsal in which they imagine themselves in a specific situation experiencing the negative consequences arising from their demanding rule. Then they can imagine switching over to their preferential rule and visualize the positive consequences of doing so. Last, but not least, helpers should assist and encourage clients to change how they communicate and act in line with their improved rules. Box 20.3 shows the revised consequences C(2) for workaholic Pat for successfully adhering to her/his improved preferential rule T(2).

Box 20.3 Example of a preferential rule and its consequences

S   Workaholic middle manager Pat reaches her/his 40th birthday and becomes highly anxious.

T(1)   *Demanding rule*

        'I must devote all my energies to my job.'

T(2)   *Preferential rule*

        'I prefer to be very competent at my job, but of equal priority is to lead a balanced life with adequate time for personal relationships and recreation.'

C(2)   *Positive feelings consequences* include less anxiety and greater happiness.

        Positive physical reactions consequences include being less tired and absence of ulcers and hypertension.

        Positive action consequences include spending less time at work yet being more productive, attending more to her/his home life, and enjoying recreation.

ACTIVITY

Activity 20.1 Assisting a client to improve a rule

Work with a partner who either uses a personal concern or role-plays a client with a mind skills goal of creating one or more preferential rules to manage a problem situation better. Within the context of a good collaborative working relationship and, possibly, using a whiteboard during the process:

- use speaking skills to describe the difference between demanding and preferential rules;
- use demonstrating skills;
- cooperate with the client to identify any major demanding rules and put the main one into the STC framework;
- use coaching skills to assist the client to question and challenge the main demanding rule;
- use coaching skills to assist the client to create a preferential rule statement to replace the demanding rule;
- together with the client anticipate the consequences of her/him managing to maintain using her/his preferential rule; and
- use negotiating homework skills.

Afterwards, discuss and reverse roles. Playing back audio recordings or video-recordings of rehearsal and practice sessions may assist learning.

21 Improving clients' perceptions

A Chinese proverb states 'Two-thirds of what we see is behind our eyes.' Clients may have systematic biases in how they interpret information. Often these biases work against their happiness and fulfillment. Helpers can closely observe how much evidence clients provide to support assertions about how they and others behave.

Perceiving and interpreting

When training clients to improve their skills at creating perceptions, helpers can start by teaching them the importance of examining the connections between how they think, feel and act. Helpers can introduce the concept of automatic thoughts or perceptions and provide an example of how underlying perceptions can influence feelings. The American psychiatrist Aaron Beck uses the example of instructing a male client to imagine a person was at home one night and heard a crash in another room. When asked how the person might react to the first interpretation 'There's a burglar in the room', the client replied that he would feel 'Very anxious, terrified' and that he might hide or phone the police. The client thought the person would react to the second interpretation 'The windows have been left open and the wind has caused something to fall over' by not being afraid, but possibly being sad if something valuable had been broken. The person would probably go and see what was the problem. Beck explained to the client that this example illustrates that there are a number of ways that people can interpret situations and that the way they interpret situations affects how they feel and behave.

Related to showing the influence of perceptions on feelings and behaviour, helpers can also train clients to understand the difference between fact and inference. Clients can learn that their perceptions of themselves, others and the world are their subjective 'facts'. Often, however, they may fail to realize that these perceptions may be based on inference rather than fact. A favourite illustration of this point by one of my Stanford University professors was: 'All Indians walk in single file . . . at least the one I saw did.' That one Indian was seen is a fact; that they all walk in single file is an inference.

Clients can make inferences about themselves, others and the environment. They can be both positive and negative. They are of varying degrees of accuracy concerning the factual data on which they are based. Box 21.1 provides two examples of the difference between fact and inference.

Box 21.1 Examples of the difference between fact and inference

Example 1

Fact: My partner fails to congratulate me effusively on the good news that I have just received a promotion.

Inference: My partner is not proud of me.

Example 2

Fact: My partner comes home late from work three evenings in a row.

Inference: She/he is more concerned with her/his career than with me.

Note: In each of the above examples, the facts and evidence did not justify the inferences.

I stress the distinction between fact and inference because it is a theme that underlies how clients create and persist in creating inaccurate perceptions. Clients may both jump to conclusions and also remain unaware that they have taken the leap. Illusion then becomes their reality, in whole or in part.

Eliciting and identifying automatic perceptions

In order to change their thinking, clients first need to become aware of their automatic perceptions. The following are some salient characteristics of such perceptions. Automatic perceptions:

- are part of people's internal monologue – what and how they talk to themselves;
- can take the form of words, images or both;
- occur very rapidly and usually at the fringe of awareness;
- can precede and accompany emotions, including feelings and inhibitions – for instance, people's emotional responses to each other's actions follow from their interpretations rather than from the actions themselves;
- are generally plausible to people who assume that they are accurate; and
- have a recurring quality, despite people trying to block them out.

Though often hard to identify, helpers can train clients to pinpoint possibly inaccurate automatic perceptions. Helpers may question clients about automatic perceptions that occur during upsetting situations. Where clients experience difficulty in recalling thoughts, helpers may use either imagery or role-playing. When questioning, helpers observe clients carefully for signs of emotion that may offer leads for further questioning. Using a whiteboard can be useful. When clients see their initial thoughts written up on the board, this may trigger them to reveal less obvious and more frightening thoughts.

Clients may be set homework assignments in which they record their thoughts and perceptions. Clients can complete daily worksheets in which they record in their separate columns:

- *Situation(s)* leading to negative emotion(s).
- *Feelings and physical reaction (s)* felt and their degree on a 0–100 scale.
- *Automatic perceptions and image(s)* and a rating of how strongly they believed the automatic perceptions(s) to be on a 0–100 scale. In addition, they can identify any particularly hot perceptions.

Helpers can also request that clients fill in worksheets identifying and rating key feelings, physical reactions, perceptions and images for specific problem situations they encounter between sessions (see Box 12.1 on page 80). Again, clients can be asked to identify hot perceptions.

Checking the accuracy of perceptions

When faced with problem situations, clients may make potentially erroneous statements about themselves, such as 'I'm no good at that', and about others, such as 'She/he always does . . .' or 'She/he never does . . .'. Such statements or perceptions influence how they feel and communicate and act. When assisting clients to check the accuracy of their perceptions, helpers are asking them to distinguish between fact and inference, and to make their inferences fit the facts as closely as possible.

Helpers can encourage clients to think of their perceptions as propositions that together they can investigate to see how far they are supported by evidence. An example provided by Aaron Beck is that of a resident who insisted 'I am not a good doctor'. Therapist and client then listed criteria for being a good doctor. The resident then monitored his behaviour and sought feedback from supervisors and colleagues. Finally, he concluded 'I am a good doctor after all'.

As shown in Box 21.2, helpers can assist clients to check the accuracy of their perceptions in problem situations by asking three main questions:

- 'Where is the evidence for your perception?'
- 'Are there any other ways of perceiving the situation?'
- 'Which way(s) of perceiving the situation best fits the available facts?'

Box 21.2 Example of checking the accuracy of a perception

Problem situation

Sophie, 31, a second-year social work student, and Chris, 34, a computer engineer, had been in an intimate relationship in Edinburgh for six months. Three months ago, Chris's company reorganized his job to a location near London. Both Sophie and Chris are still emotionally involved with one another, phone and email regularly, and Chris has gone back to Edinburgh once and plans to go again soon. However, the course of true love is not going smoothly. In a recent telephone conversation Chris informed Sophie that he had been to visit a former girlfriend, Amanda, 28, a couple of times in hospital where she was recovering from her injuries as a result of a serious car accident. At this news Sophie became extremely anxious and upset with Chris, who now feels very hurt and thinks that she neither trusts nor understands him.

Potentially erroneous perception

'Chris is more interested in Amanda and does not love me anymore.'

Question 1 'Where is the evidence for your perception?'

When asked this question, Sophie says she has no real evidence. When they were seeing each other regularly in Edinburgh, Chris never behaved in a way that suggested he was cheating on her. Chris had told her long ago about Amanda, that his relationship with her had been platonic, and that they broke off by mutual agreement.

Question 2 'Are there any other ways of perceiving the situation?'

Sophie and her helper come up with the following different perceptions:

- 'Amanda is trying to use her injuries as a way of ensnaring Chris back into a relationship.'
- 'If Chris were more involved with Amanda than me, he would not have told me about going to see her in hospital.'
- 'I've had a heavy cold recently which has made me feel under the weather.'
- 'Chris going to see Amanda in hospital shows that he is a caring guy, which is one of the main things I love about him.'
- 'Chris is feeling lonely down near London and is looking for more female company.'

Question 3 'Which way(s) of perceiving the situation best fits the available facts?'

After some thought, Sophie decides that the most accurate perceptions are:

- 'If Chris were more involved with Amanda than me, he would not have told me about going to see her in hospital.'
- 'I've had a heavy cold recently which has made me feel under the weather.'
- 'Chris going to see Amanda in hospital shows that he is a caring guy, which is one of the main things I love about him.'

Irrational jealousy can be a big problem in close relationships. In the example in Box 21.2, Sophie is fortunate enough to have a helper who, in the context of a good collaborative relationship, helps her to gain insight into a potentially dangerous automatic perception. Had Sophie persisted in her automatic perception, which left her prone to self-pity and being aggressive towards Chris, she might well have lost him. The result of Sophie thinking more deeply about her automatic perception was that she calmed down and managed to get her relationship with Chris back on an even keel. Chris then gladly went ahead with his planned Edinburgh visit.

Helpers can go beyond assisting clients to change single inaccurate automatic perceptions, to make them more aware that they may have a tendency to process information in biased ways. For instance, in future, when faced with similar feelings of self-doubt and jealousy, Sophie could use the skills of questioning herself to test the reality of her perceptions. Helpers may also need to assist clients to alter thoughts in more than one mind skills area. For instance, a helper might encourage Sophie to challenge and alter a demanding rule such as 'My boyfriend must never be friendly with other women.' Furthermore, Sophie could learn to use calming and coaching self-talk to guide her in communicating assertively rather than aggressively on future occasions when she wishes to discuss sensitive issues with Chris.

ACTIVITY

Activity 21.1 Assisting a client to test the reality of a perception

Work with a partner who either uses a personal concern or role-plays a client with a goal of creating one or more realistic perception(s) to manage a problem situation better. Within the context of a good collaborative working relationship and, possibly, using a whiteboard during the process:

- use speaking skills to describe the importance of reality-testing perceptions rather than jumping to conclusions;
- use demonstrating skills;
- cooperate with the client to identify a possibly inaccurate automatic perception concerning the situation;
- help your client to test the reality of the automatic perception by asking her/him the questions:

- – 'Where is the evidence for your perception?'
- – 'Are there any other ways of perceiving the situation?'
- – 'Which way(s) of perceiving the situation best fits the available facts?'; and
• use negotiating homework skills.

Afterwards, discuss and reverse roles. Playing back audio recordings or video-recordings of rehearsal and practice sessions may assist learning.

22   Negotiating homework

The theme of this chapter is that of how, during helping, clients can use the time in between contacts with their helpers to best effect. On many occasions helpers may find it useful to discuss with clients homework activities that they might undertake before they meet again. In formal counselling these would be between session activities. Here I use the term 'negotiating homework' because of the large variety of settings and ways in which helping takes place. In some settings the word 'homework' might be considered stuffy or inappropriate because of its educational connotations. If so, helpers can use different terminology that works best for them and their clients. For the sake of simplicity, much of the following discussion on negotiating homework assumes formal helping sessions. Consequently, readers for whom this assumption is inaccurate should adapt the discussion to their special circumstances.

Negotiating homework

After presenting, demonstrating and coaching clients in improved ways of thinking and communicating/acting, in the context of collaborative working relationships helpers and clients can negotiate relevant homework assignments. Homework assignments include trying out changed behaviours in real life and filling out self-monitoring sheets and worksheets for developing mind skills that influence feelings, communications and actions. Other assignments can entail reading self-help books, listening to cassettes, watching videotapes and observing people with good communication skills.

Many reasons exist for suggesting to clients that they perform homework assignments. These reasons include speeding up the learning process and encouraging clients to monitor, rehearse and practice changed communications and actions. Furthermore, homework activities can help the transfer of behaviours worked on in helping to real life. Sometimes, when this happens, clients experience difficulties in applying their improved behaviours. Such difficulties may be addressed when next meeting their helpers. In addition, homework assignments can increase clients' sense of self-control and of personal responsibility for improving how they think, communicate and act.

One of the central problems in assigning homework activities is getting clients to do them. Often as a counsellor trainer I have observed students rush through negotiating homework assignments at the end of helping sessions in ways that virtually guaranteed client non-compliance. Common mistakes included not leaving enough time, inviting insufficient client participation, giving vague verbal instructions, and not checking whether clients clearly understood what they were meant to do. Box 22.1 lists nine guidelines recommended by prominent American cognitive therapists Christine Padesky and Dennis Greenberger for increasing the chances of client compliance.

Box 22.1 Guidelines for increasing clients' compliance with homework assignments

1 Make assignments small.
2 Assign tasks within the clients' skill level.
3 Make assignments relevant and interesting.
4 Collaborate with the client in developing learning assignments.
5 Provide a clear rationale for the assignment and a written summary.
6 Begin the assignment during the session.
7 Identify and problem solve impediments to the assignment.
8 Emphasize learning, not a desired outcome.
9 Show interest, and follow up in the next appointment.

Helpers can design their own homework assignment forms or write down tailor-made instructions as occasion arises. These may be either the best or only options for informal helping contexts. Box 22.2 presents four formats for homework forms based on the assumption of formal helping sessions. Where possible, either helper or client should write down clear instructions for homework assignments on these forms. Writing instructions on scraps of paper is generally not good enough. Helpers should always check what clients write to make sure they have taken down the instructions correctly. If helpers want clients to fill out forms such as monitoring logs, they should provide these forms themselves. This practice ensures clear instructions and saves clients the extra effort of having to write out forms before filling them in.

Box 22.2 Formats for homework forms

Format 1

Homework assignment form

In order to gain the most from your helping session(s) you are encouraged to engage in the following between session activities.

Format 2

To Follow Up

In order to gain the most from your helping session(s) you are encouraged to perform the following tasks.

Format 3

Take Away Sheet

Use this sheet for writing down (1) your main learnings from helping and (2) any instructions for between session activities.

Format 4

Learning Contract

I make a learning contract with myself to perform the following activities before the next helping session.

Note: As appropriate, substitute the word 'counselling' for 'helping'.

Sometimes, changing a way of communicating or acting requires clients to give up long established habits. Here, it can be especially important for helpers and clients not to agree on too difficult an activity too soon. Where possible, they should try to build in some early successes to encourage clients to persist in working on their skills.

Some clients return to non-supportive, if not downright hostile environments. If so, helpers may need to prepare clients more thoroughly prior to suggesting that they implement their improved communications and actions outside of helping. Such preparation may include devising strategies for coping with negative feedback.

Lastly, helpers should signal a joint progress review by letting clients know that, when they next meet, they will ask them how they fared in their homework assignments. Clients who know that their helpers are interested in and supportive of their attempts to complete homework assignments are more likely to be motivated to do so, that is so long as these helpers avoid becoming controlling and judgmental.

Identifying supports and resources

The need to identify supports and resources outside of helping overlaps with that of negotiating homework with clients. Both focus on assisting clients to use time well outside of helping. Helpers may need to raise some clients' awareness about the importance of identifying and using supports and of lessening contact with non-supportive people. Helpers can assist clients to identify people in their home environments who can support their efforts to improve how they think, communicate and act. For example, a client with a drinking problem might be encouraged to join Alcoholics Anonymous. Another example is helping university students with poor study skills to seek out sympathetic lecturers and tutors to assist them, for instance, in writing more polished essays or revising well for examinations. Unemployed people can approach friends and relatives who may not only offer them emotional support but also be sources for job leads. Women working on verbal, vocal and body messages for communicating more assertively can seek out women's groups where they may find other women with similar objectives.

An inverse approach to support is for helpers to assist clients in identifying unsympathetic or counterproductive people. Clients are then left with various choices: getting such people to accept, if not support, their efforts to change; seeing less of them; or stopping seeing them altogether. If these people are family members, avoiding them altogether may be difficult, especially if clients are financially dependent on them. Here, helpers and clients may discuss damage control strategies. However, clients can often choose their friendship and membership groups and therefore may be able to change the company they keep.

Helpers may enlist a variety of people as aides, such as partners, teachers, parents, welfare workers, supervisors and friends. Some guidelines for using third parties as helpers' aides include obtaining the permission of clients, identifying suitable people and, where necessary, training them in their roles. An example of using third parties as aides is that of asking teachers to help shy and lonely pupils to participate more in class.

In addition, helpers can assist clients to identify and use resources for helping them attain and maintain improved ways of thinking, communicating and acting. Such resources include workshops and short courses, self-help books and manuals, instructional audio-cassettes, videotapes and CD-ROMs, appropriate voluntary agencies, peer support groups and networks, telephone hot-lines and crisis information outlets.

Helpers should familiarize themselves with and establish contact with the human supports and educational and information resources of most relevance to the client populations with which they work. Access to suitable supports and resources may be of tremendous assistance to some clients as they take positive steps towards changing how they think, communicate and act in problem areas.

ACTIVITIES

Activity 22.1 Negotiating homework

Work with a partner who selects a problem situation in which she or he wants to communicate better. Collaborate with your partner to identify some key verbal, vocal and body messages in need of improvement. Using coaching, demonstrating and rehearsing, assist your partner to improve her/his skills. Then rehearse and practise how to negotiate one or more homework activities so that your partner can use the time (assume a week) before you next meet to good effect. To increase your clients' chances of compliance, observe the following guidelines:

- allow adequate time for negotiating homework;
- introduce the idea that practising between helping sessions is important;
- negotiate rather than impose activities;
- ensure that the activities are realistic;
- ensure that your client knows precisely what to do;
- get the instructions written down accurately;
- discuss potential difficulties in completing agreed upon activities; and
- signal a joint progress review.

Afterwards, hold a sharing and discussion session focused on the helper's use of negotiating homework skills. If necessary, allow the helper to practise some more until the helper considers that she/he has obtained some degree of competence in negotiating homework.
Then, if feasible, reverse roles.

Activity 22.2 Identifying supports and resources

For the client population(s) with whom you either work or might work with in future, identify:

1 What kinds of people might support your clients' attempts to change?
2 What kinds of non-human resources (for instance, cassettes or self-help books) might support your clients' attempts to change?

23 Conducting middle sessions

This chapter is relevant to those helpers who either use or are likely to use their counselling skills in settings where it is possible to conduct a series of formal helping sessions. Nevertheless, I hope that readers who use counselling skills in either informal helping contacts or as part of other primary roles can also find something of value from it. The focus here is on middle sessions, those that take place after the initial session and before the last session. If anything, the following review focuses more on conducting sessions in the improving communications/actions and thoughts approach than the facilitating problem solving approach to the changing stage of the RUC helping model. However, many points are relevant to both approaches.

Helping sessions have four phases: preparing, starting, middle and ending. In Box 23.1, based on the assumption that helping will continue for at least one more session, some relevant skills are listed for each phase.

Box 23.1 The four phases of helping sessions

1 The preparing phase
Illustrative skills

Reflecting on previous and next session(s).

Consulting with trainers, supervisors and peers.

Understanding how to improve the targeted communications/actions and thoughts.

Arriving on time.

Setting up the room.

Relaxing oneself.

2 The starting phase
Illustrative skills

Meeting, greeting and seating.

Re-establishing the collaborative working relationship.

Reviewing homework.

Establishing session agendas.

3 The middle phase
Illustrative skills

Actively involving clients in the change process.

Coaching, demonstrating and rehearsing.

Checking clients' understanding.

Refining session agendas.

Keeping sessions moving.

4 The ending phase
Illustrative skills

Structuring to allow time for ending.

Reviewing sessions.

Negotiating homework.

Arranging subsequent contact.

The preparing phase

Adequate preparation of helping sessions is very important. Helpers should arrive either early or on time for sessions, make sure the room is in order, check any recording equipment they might use and, if necessary, relax themselves. In most instances helper should not allow clients into interview rooms before they are ready to devote their full attention to them.

Where appropriate, supervisors, trainers and colleagues can assist helpers to review the previous session to gain insights into how they might approach the next one. In addition, helpers can revise any strategies they intend using in order to understand their content thoroughly. If necessary, helpers can also practise delivering the strategies. Furthermore, helpers can use between-session time to ensure that they have any written material, such as handouts and homework forms, readily available. However, helpers should avoid being too rigid in approaching sessions since consulting with clients is part of establishing good collaborative working relationships.

The starting phase

The starting phase has three main tasks: re-establishing a collaborative working relationship, reviewing homework, and establishing a session agenda. Once clients are comfortably seated, sometimes they will start talking of their own accord. However, on most occasions, helpers need to make an opening statement. Sample opening statements are provided in Box 23.2. I advocate a 'softly, softly' approach that starts by checking 'where the client is at' rather than by moving directly into improving behaviour. Helpers should allow clients the psychological safety and space to bring them up to date with information that they select as important from their internal frames of reference.

Once helpers have allowed clients air time, they may still require further information to help them to assess how clients have progressed in any homework negotiated in the previous session. Box 23.2 provides some statements that helpers might make, if they have not already reviewed progress in doing the homework. As appropriate, helpers can ask additional questions that clarify and expand their own and clients' understanding of how they are progressing. Furthermore, helpers can encourage clients to acknowledge their conscious involvement, or personal agency, in bringing about positive changes during homework. For example, Sid, a production line supervisor, was prone to angry outbursts with Ben, a young management trainee whom he perceived as a know-all. Sid, who has now restrained his anger, says 'Things are going better in our relationship.' Sid's helper encourages him to acknowledge that by changing his behaviour, for instance, by replacing negative with calming self-talk, he has helped to bring about the improvement. Sid might now say to himself 'If I use my self-talk skills, then I can restrain my anger and improve my working relationship with Ben.'

Near the start of each session in the changing stage, helpers should consult with clients to establish session agendas. Such agendas may be for all or part of sessions. For example, together they may decide what they will work on first and then, later, make another decision regarding what to work on next. Alternatively, as part of their initial agenda-setting discussion, they may target one area to start and then agree to move on to another area. However, both helpers and clients should be flexible once they establish session agendas so that they can respond to emerging developments during sessions.

When establishing session agendas, I favour paying considerable attention to clients' wishes, since I want to encourage their motivation and involvement. If I thought there was some important reason for starting with a particular improving communication or thoughts goal, I would share this observation. However, I would still be inclined to allow clients the final say in determining the agenda. Box 23.2 illustrates the kind of agenda-setting statement that helpers might make near the start of second sessions. Session agendas for later sessions tend to be heavily influenced by the work done and homework negotiated in the previous session.

Box 23.2 Some examples of starting phase statements

Opening statements
'How's your week been?'

'How have you been getting on?'

'Where would you like to start today?'

Reviewing homework
'What progress did you make with your homework?'

'What happened when you tried out your changed thoughts/ communications?'

'Things didn't just happen, you made them happen by changing [specify what].'

Establishing a session agenda

'In our first session we stated two changing thinking goals for developing your telephone dating skills: namely, using coping rather than negative self-talk and challenging and then replacing your demanding rule about needing everyone's approval. We also stated some goals for improving the verbal and vocal message components of how you communicate on the phone. What would you like to work on first?'

The middle phase

Once session agendas are established, however informally, helpers can use strategies to assist clients to attain one or more goals. One way of viewing this middle phase is that it is the working phase of the session. However, I have not used the term 'working phase' because it may detract from valuable work performed in the preparing, starting and ending phases.

I have already emphasized the importance of client-centred coaching when assisting clients to improve their skills. In the middle phase, helpers can involve clients in choices that take place when working on specific skills, for instance, how many rehearsals they require to develop targeted verbal, vocal and body messages. Furthermore, helpers can involve clients in choices about moving on to different items in their session agendas and refining agendas as appropriate. Together, they may make trade-offs and compromises regarding spending session time: for instance, curtailing time spent in one mind skill's or communication skill's area so that they have time available for another.

Helpers need to keep helping sessions moving at an appropriate pace, neither too fast nor too slow. There are risks in both directions. On the one hand, they may rush through delivering helping strategies in ways that confuse clients and leave them little to take away after a session's end. Furthermore, helpers may put too much pressure on clients to reveal themselves and to work at uncongenial paces.

On the other hand, helpers may allow 'session drift' – sessions that drift along rather aimlessly with little tangible outcome being achieved. Sometimes session drift occurs because helpers are poor at balancing relationship and task considerations, at the expense of the latter. They may need to develop assertion skills to curtail long and unproductive conversations. Furthermore, they require a repertoire of checking-out and moving-on statements. Box 23.3 provides examples of such statements.

Though the responsibility should be shared, ultimately it is the helper's responsibility to see that session time is allocated productively. Helpers should be careful not to make moving on statements that allow insufficient time to deal with the next agenda items properly. Generally, it is best to avoid getting into new areas towards the end of sessions rather than to start working on them in rushed and hurried ways.

Box 23.3 Examples of statements for the middle and ending phases

Middle phase statements

'Do you want to spend more time now working in this area or are you ready to move on?'

'I sense that we've taken working on changing your . . . [specify] as far as we can for now, what do you think?'

'Do you want another rehearsal for communicating better in that situation or do you think you can manage all right?'

Ending phase statements

'I notice that we have to end in about ten minutes . . . and, assuming you want to come here again, perhaps we should spend some of this time looking at what you might do before our next meeting.'

'Before we end it might be a good idea to review what we've done today and see how you can build upon it before we next meet.'

'Is there anything you would like to bring up before we end?'

The ending phase

There are various tasks involved in ending sessions skillfully in the changing stage of the RUC helping model. Helpers need to bring closure to any work on a targeted skill in process during the middle phase. They may want to have either themselves or their clients review sessions. If clients have not done so already, this may be an opportunity for them to write down their main learnings. In addition, helpers should leave sufficient time to negotiate and clarify any homework that clients will undertake. Furthermore, helpers and clients should discuss and be clear about arrangements for their next session.

To allow time to perform the tasks of the ending phase properly, often it is a good idea to make an early structuring statement that allows for a smooth transition from the middle to the ending phase of the session. You might make such a statement about 5 to 10 minutes before the end of a 45-minute session. The first two ending phase statements in Box 23.3 are examples of statements helpers might make in this regard.

Sometimes reviewing sessions helps clients to clarify and consolidate what they have learned in them. However, session reviews are not always necessary, especially if helpers and clients have worked thoroughly during the session. Furthermore, when helpers negotiate homework they may cover some of the same ground anyway.

In the previous chapter, I mentioned some ways of increasing clients' compliance in performing homework activities. At risk of repetition, these ways include negotiating them rather than imposing them, checking that clients clearly know how to enact the changed thoughts and communications, writing activities instructions and key points down, and discussing with clients any difficulties that they anticipate in carrying out the activities.

When ending sessions, helpers may also check whether clients have any unfinished business, queries or outstanding items that they would like to mention. Some helpers like to check how clients have experienced the session and whether they have any feedback they would like to share with them. Lastly, helpers should make clear agreements with clients about whether and when they are next going to meet. Helpers may also wish to tell vulnerable 'at risk' clients under what circumstances and how they can contact them between sessions.

ACTIVITY

Activity 23.1 Practising conducting second sessions

Work with a partner. Partner A acts as a helper and partner B as the client. The client chooses a problem situation of relevance to her/him. Assume that you have conducted an initial session in which helper and client have completed the first two stages of the Relating–Understanding–Changing helping model. Furthermore, assume that you and your client have identified at least one communication/action and at least one thought to be improved during the changing stage, which may last for at least one more session after this one. Since this is not a real second session, you will need to discuss how each of you can best get into your roles.

Then conduct a second helping session consisting of the following four phases:

- preparing phase (this may include addressing issues connected with your respective roles);
- starting phase;
- middle phase; and
- ending phase.

Afterwards, hold a sharing and feedback discussion. Then, if appropriate, change roles and repeat this activity.

Using audio cassette or videotape recording and playback may add value to the activity.

24   Terminating helping

This chapter deals with issues connected with terminating and conducting final sessions. As with the previous chapter, it is mainly based on the assumption that helpers have the opportunity to work with clients over a series of sessions, say three or more. Again, I hope those readers for whom this assumption does not hold, because of the different nature of their client contacts, are able to gain something of value from the discussion.

When to terminate

Within the Relating–Understanding–Changing model, when do helpers terminate the helping process? Sometimes clients may terminate of their own accord before helpers think they are ready. Though this may be either because of a helper–client mismatch or because helpers demonstrated insufficient skill to have them return, this is not necessarily the case. Clients may have found their session or sessions with helpers of value, but think they can continue on their own. Sometimes, external circumstances such as a change of job or illness may prevent them continuing. In addition, some clients just resist the ideas of having to change and of being in helping.

Many problem situations have their own time frames. When helping clients handle specific future events, clients may only wish to continue up until that event. In informal helping, contact may end when clients leave settings such as hospitals and residential units for juvenile delinquents. On other occasions, helping may terminate when clients have made sufficient progress in either the facilitating problem solving or the improving communications/actions and thoughts approaches to the third stage of the RUC model.

The following are four main sources of information that helpers and clients can use in reviewing when to terminate helping. First, there is information from what clients report about their feelings and progress. Are they happy with progress and do they feel they can cope better? Second, there are helpers' own observations about clients' progress. Third, there is feedback from significant others in clients' lives, for instance, spouses, bosses or peers. Sometimes this feedback goes direct to clients and then gets relayed to helpers. Last, helpers and clients may terminate helping on the basis of evidence of attaining measurable goals. An example might be that of a single mother and teenaged son previously in conflict who report having ten minutes of 'happy talk' each day for a week, the son mowed the lawn as agreed, and the mother expressed love and appreciation at least once each day.

Formats for terminating helping

Sometimes helpers and clients have limited choice over when to terminate. Such instances include when clients leave town, when terms end, and when helping addresses specific forthcoming situations such as important examinations or a divorce hearing. On other occasions, helpers and clients have more choice about when to terminate. The following are some possible formats for terminating helping:

- *Fixed termination* Helpers and clients may have contracts that they work for, say, eight sessions in one or more problem or problematic skills areas. Advantages of fixed termination include lessening the chance of dependency and motivating clients to use helping to best effect. Potential disadvantages include restricting coverage of problems and insufficient thoroughness in training clients to improve specific skills.
- *Open termination when goals are attained* With open terminations, helping concludes when helpers and clients agree that clients have made sufficient progress in attaining their main goals. Such goals include managing specific problems better and developing improved skills to address current and future problems.
- *Faded termination* Here the withdrawal of helping assistance is gradual. For example, instead of meeting weekly, the final sessions could be at fortnightly or monthly intervals.
- *Terminating with booster session(s)* Booster sessions, say after three months, are not to teach new skills, but to check clients' progress in

consolidating skills, motivate them, and help them work through difficulties in taking away and using trained skills in their home environments.

*   *Scheduling follow-up contact after ending* Helpers can schedule follow-up phone calls or postal and email correspondence with clients. Such phone calls and correspondence perform some of the same functions as booster sessions.

Assisting maintaining change

Issues surrounding maintaining changes in problem situations should not be left to final sessions. Helpers can assist clients to maintain changes during helping by identifying the key mind and communication skills clients need to develop, training thoroughly and negotiating relevant homework that helps clients to transfer what they have learned inside helping to problem situations outside.

During helping, helpers may make statements indicating its finiteness: for instance, comments about the usefulness of homework for developing improved skills for use when helping ends. Such comments may encourage clients to make the most of their regular sessions and the time between them. Helpers can also introduce the topic of termination with one or more transition statements that clearly signal that helping is coming to an end. Box 24.1 provides examples of such transition statements.

Box 24.1 Examples of transition statements for terminating helping

'We only have a few more sessions left. Perhaps we should not only discuss an agenda for this session, but think about how best we can spend our remaining time together.'

'Our next session is the final session. Would it be all right with you if we spent some time discussing how to help you retain and build on your improved skills for managing your problem?'

'Perhaps the agenda for this final session should mainly be how to help you use the skills you've learned here for afterwards. For instance, we can review how much you've changed, where there is still room for improvement, how you might go about it, and plan how to deal with any difficult situations you anticipate.'

The main task in terminating helping is to assist clients to consolidate what they have learned so that they may continue to help themselves afterwards. One method of enhancing consolidation is for either helper or client to summarize the main points learned for dealing with problem situations in future. In addition, helpers and clients can spend time anticipating difficulties and setbacks and develop strategies for dealing with them. Some of these strategies may be focused on communication: for instance, how to seek support during attempts to handle a difficult problem situation better.

Helpers can stress the importance of clients understanding that often they can retrieve mistakes and always they can learn from them. Together, helpers and clients can develop appropriate self-talk statements for retrieving lapses and get them written down on reminder cards. Furthermore, helpers can prevent discouragement by distinguishing between a process success and an outcome success: even though clients have used good skills in a problem situation (a process success) they may not get what they want (an outcome success). Not getting what they want does not negate the fact that they still performed competently and can do so again in future.

In addition, where appropriate, helpers can challenge clients' demanding rules that 'change must be easy' and 'maintaining change must be effortless'. Helpers should encourage clients to replace such rules with more preferential rules stressing that changing and maintaining change can involve effort, practise and overcoming obstacles. Helpers can also emphasize clients' assuming personal responsibility for continuing to cope with their problem situations to the best of their ability.

Sometimes it is appropriate for helpers to explore with clients some arrangements for continuing support. Such support may take the form of identifying and using supportive people, referral to another helper, attending a helping group or training course, self-help reading, and self-help audio cassettes or videotapes. In addition, as mentioned previously, helpers can offer review and booster sessions.

Further terminating helping tasks and skills

In addition to the major task of consolidating improved behaviours, there are other tasks when terminating helping. How helpers handle them varies with length of helping, the nature of problem(s) and problematic skills, and the helper–client relationship.

Dealing with feelings

Clients' feelings when terminating helping fall into two main categories: feelings about how they are going to fare without helpers and feelings toward helpers and the helping process. Some clients have feelings of ambivalence about how they will cope after helping. On the one hand they feel more competent, yet on the other hand they still have doubts about their abilities to implement skills. Helpers can facilitate open discussion of such clients' feelings about the future. Looking at how best to maintain skills also addresses the issue of clients' lingering doubts. Other clients will feel confident that they can cope now on their own, which is hopefully a sign of work well done.

Helpers should allow clients the opportunity to share feelings about their contact with them. They may obtain valuable feedback about both how they come across and clients' reactions to different aspects of the helping process. Helpers may humanize terminating by sharing some of their feelings with clients: for instance, 'I enjoyed working with you', 'I admire the courage with which you face your situation' or 'I'm delighted with your progress.'

Terminating helping ethically

Helpers should aim to say goodbye in a businesslike yet friendly way, appropriate to professional rather than personal relationships. By ending helping sloppily, helpers may undo some of their influence in helping clients to maintain their skills.

There are a number of important ethical issues surrounding terminating helping. For example, helpers need to think through their responsibilities to clients after helping. Too much support may engender dependency, too little may fail to carry out professional obligations. Each case must be judged on its own merits. Another ethical issue is what helpers should do when they think that clients have other problems on which they need to work. I suggest tactfully bringing such views to clients' attention.

A further set of ethical issues surrounds the boundaries between personal and professional relationships. Most professional associations have ethical codes about providing counselling and helping services. Helpers who allow their personal and professional wires to get crossed when terminating are not only acting unethically, but can make it more difficult for clients to be assisted by them if future need arises.

Evaluating counselling skills

When helping terminates, helpers have many sources of information for evaluating their counselling skills. These sources of information include attendance, intentional and unintentional feedback from clients, perceptions of client progress, session notes, possibly videotapes or audiocassettes of helping sessions, clients' compliance and success in carrying out homework, and feedback from third parties such as supervisors.

Helpers can make a final evaluation of their work with each client soon after terminating regular contact. Questions helpers can ask include: 'To what extent did the client manage her/his problem(s) better and improve her/his skills?' and 'How well did I use the skills for each stage of the Relating–Understanding–Changing model?' If helpers defer performing such an evaluation for too long, they risk forgetting valuable information. When evaluating their counselling skills, helpers should be aware of their characteristic perceiving errors: for example, they may be too hard or too easy on themselves. What they seek is a balanced appraisal of their good and poor skills to guide their work with future clients.

ACTIVITIES

Activity 24.1 Considerations in terminating helping

1 Critically discuss the importance and validity of each of the following considerations for when helping should terminate:
   • client self-report;
   • helper observations;
   • third-party feedback;
   • attainment of measurable goals; and
   • other factors not mentioned above.
2 Critically discuss the merits of each of the following formats for terminating helping:
   • fixed ending decided in the initial session; and
   • open ending negotiated between client and helper.
3 Critically discuss the value of each of the following ways of assisting clients to maintain their improved behaviours:
   • summarizing the main learnings;
   • anticipating difficulties and setbacks and developing strategies for dealing with them;
   • focusing on how clients can think effectively after helping;
   • exploring arrangements for continuing support; and
   • other ways not mentioned above.

Activity 24.2 Terminating a series of helping sessions

Work with the same partner with whom you performed Activity 23.1. Again, partner A acts as a helper and partner B acts as the client. For the problem situation worked on in Activity 23.1, assume that you are now in your third and final helping session. Conduct all or part of this final helping session in which you focus on:

- assisting your client to maintain changes;
- terminating helping smoothly; and
- saying goodbye.

Afterwards, hold a sharing and feedback discussion. Then, if appropriate, change roles and repeat this activity.

Using audio cassette or videotape recording and playback may add value to the activity.

PART III

Further considerations

25 Multicultural and gender-aware helping

This chapter provides a brief introduction to diversity-sensitive help-ing. Addressing the range of differences presented in Chapter 4 is much too vast a topic for a single chapter. Consequently, I review issues con-nected with multicultural helping and gender-aware helping as being particularly important and relevant to many helpers and their clients. Since gender roles are one of the principal ways in which cultures differ, frequently multicultural helping and gender-aware helping overlap.

Multicultural helping

Multicultural helping goals

There are many different client groups for whom cultural considera-tions are important. These groupings include indigenous people, such as Australian Aborigines and Torres Strait Islanders, first generation migrants, descendents of migrants at varying levels of assimilation to the mainstream culture, and members of the mainstream culture, among others.

Sometimes the goals of multicultural helping are simplified to that of how best to assist minority group members when faced with hostile majority group cultures. In reality, multicultural helping is a much more complex and varied endeavour. Some goals for multicultural helping centre around the period of transition from a previous culture to a new host culture, such as that of Britain and Australia. Many migrants require culture-sensitive support to help them adjust and assimilate into their new host cultures. A minority of migrants require specialized help for post-traumatic stress disorders caused by their previous home country and refugee experiences, some of which were horrific.

Another set of goals for multicultural helping concerns issues of equality, self-respect and coping with discrimination. Helpers can assist clients to take pride in their culture and race and to liberate themselves from internalized negative stereotypes. Some clients require support and skills to deal with the inner wounds and outer circumstances of racism. Furthermore, some mainstream culture clients require assistance in relinquishing negative aspects of their upbringing, such as a false sense of cultural and racial superiority.

Multicultural counselling competencies

Increasingly helpers are challenged to develop multicultural counselling competencies. A committee of the American Psychological Association's Division of Counseling Psychology has identified multicultural counselling competencies as having three main dimensions: awareness of own assumptions, values and biases; understanding the worldview of the culturally different client; and developing appropriate strategies and techniques (see Sue et al., *Multicultural Counseling Competencies* in the Annotated Bibliography). Each dimension is divided into beliefs and attitudes, knowledge and skills. Readers may feel overwhelmed when reading about the proposed multicultural competencies, since it is a counsel of perfection. However, I present a summary of the competencies to indicate some areas that helpers may need to address when using basic counselling skills with people from different cultures.

Awareness of own assumptions, values and biases

The beliefs held by culturally skilled counsellors include being sensitive to their own cultural heritage, being comfortable with the differences of clients from other cultures and races, and recognizing the limitations of their competence and expertise. Counsellors should know about their cultural and racial heritage and how this affects the therapeutic process, understand how oppression, racism and discrimination may affect them personally and in their work, and know about the impact of how they communicate on culturally different clients. Skills include seeking out relevant educational and training experiences, actively understanding oneself as a cultural and racial being, and seeking an identity that transcends race.

Understanding the worldview of the culturally different client

Beliefs and attitudes for culturally skilled counsellors include being aware of their negative emotional reactions and of the stereotypes and preconceived notions that they may hold towards culturally and racially different groups. Counsellors should know about the cultural experiences, cultural heritage and historical backgrounds of any particular group with whom they work, acknowledge how culture and race can affect help-seeking behaviour, know how culture and race can influence assessment and the selection and implementation of counselling interventions, and know about the oppressive political and environmental influences impinging on the lives of ethnic and racial minorities. Skills include keeping up to date on research findings relevant to the psychological wellbeing of various ethnic and racial groups as well as being actively involved with minorities outside of work settings to gain deeper insight into their perspectives.

Developing appropriate intervention strategies and techniques

Culturally skilled counsellors' attitudes and beliefs include respecting clients' religious and spiritual beliefs about physical and mental functioning, respecting indigenous helping practices, and valuing bilingualism. Their knowledge base includes understanding how the culture-bound, class-bound and monolingual characteristics of counselling clash with the cultural values of various minority groups, being aware of institutional barriers to minority groups using helping services, knowing about the potential for bias in assessment instruments, and understanding minority group family structures, hierarchies and community characteristics and resources. Skills include the ability to send and receive verbal and non-verbal communication accurately, interacting in the language requested by clients or making appropriate referrals, tailoring the counselling relationship and interventions to the clients' stage of cultural and racial identity development, and engaging in a variety of helping roles beyond those perceived as conventional for counsellors. Such roles include adviser, advocate, change agent and facilitator of indigenous healing and support systems.

Beginning helpers need to build their skills cumulatively, from the basic to the more advanced. They cannot be expected to have expertise at dealing with a range of culturally different clients that even many experienced helpers do not possess. Gaining an initial awareness of how cultural considerations can influence basic counselling skills, such as active listening and asking questions, is a good place to start in the process of developing into genuinely culturally sensitive helpers.

Gender-aware helping

Gender-aware helping goals

Where gender role issues are involved, it is possible to state helping goals for both sexes and for each sex. Gender-aware helping for both sexes involves general goals that include assisting individual clients to use their strengths and potential, make appropriate choices, remedy poor skills and develop positive and flexible self-concepts. In addition, helping goals relating to gender roles can often involve both male and female partners: for example, learning to deal with demand/withdraw interaction patterns in marital conflict and handling the numerous issues confronting dual career couples in a time of rapid technological and economic change.

Essential goals for feminist counselling and helping are women valuing themselves on their own terms and women becoming free of sex-role stereotypes. Statements of goals that take women's sex and gender issues into account can focus both on women's life span issues and on problems that are much more commonly faced by women than men. For example, gender-aware and feminist helpers can counsel mid-life women to cope with the menopause constructively. In addition, suitably trained and qualified helpers can assist women to address issues such as insufficient assertion, eating disorders, domestic violence and sexual harassment.

Helping goals for men can include addressing excessive need for success, power and competition, restrictive emotionality, and restrictive affectionate behaviour between men. Other helping goals for men clients include stopping being physically violent both inside and outside of the home, dealing with work-related stress, overcoming tendencies to treat women as sexual objects and developing better healthcare skills. Since women are redefining their gender roles faster than men, many men are then put in positions of exploring, understanding and altering their own gender roles. Positive maleness, combining tenderness and toughness and treating women with respect and as equals, is a desirable outcome from this change process.

Gender-aware helping approaches

Undoubtedly the rise of feminism and the start of a men's movement have already influenced many helpers of both sexes to undertake counselling and helping with a greater focus on healing psychological distress stemming from restrictive gender role socialization and sexism.

Earlier in this chapter, I presented a statement of multicultural counselling competencies. This statement can be adapted for gender aware counselling competencies which consist of three main dimensions: awareness of own assumptions, values and biases; understanding the worldview of the sex-different client; and developing appropriate strategies and techniques. The basic assumption in stating these competencies is that all helpers need to address their own levels of gender awareness and their ability to offer gender sensitive services.

Feminist counselling and helping is a prominent approach to addressing gender issues. Feminist helpers subscribe to many different theoretical orientations. Feminist helping is perhaps best described by the values or principles that have emerged from the joining of feminism with counselling. Box 25.1 describes five such central principles underlying feminist helping.

Box 25.1 Five central principles of feminist helping

1 **Egalitarian relationships** Feminist helpers are extremely sensitive to issues of power and its distribution. They emphasize sharing power with clients and believe that hierarchical forms of power distribution are inappropriate. Self-disclosure of one's own experiences as a woman can be an important part of the counselling process.

2 **Pluralism** Feminist theory acknowledges and values difference, including complex and multiple-level diversities. Respect for others, including their differences, is a basic tenet of feminist helping.

3 **Working against oppression** Feminist helpers work against all forms of oppression: for instance, on the basis of sex, sexual/ affectionate orientation, race, culture, religious belief, lifestyle choice and physical disability.

4 **External emphasis** External factors, such as social/political/ economic structures, are crucial to shaping the views of women, how they see themselves and how others see them. Women as individuals are shaped by and interact with political, environmental, institutional and cultural factors.

5   **Valuing women's experiences** Relying on the actual experiences of women for descriptions of 'reality'. Grounding knowledge claimed about women on women's actual experience. Valuing highly the experience of women rather than ignoring or discounting it and assuming men's experience to be normative.

What are some specific interventions in dealing with women clients? Interventions commonly cited by feminist helpers include challenging sex-role stereotypes, challenging patriarchal norms, assertiveness training, strategies to encourage a sense of empowerment, and self-disclosure. Needless to say, many women clients bring to helping specific problems for which gender-related strategies can be, but not always are, irrelevant.

An issue in feminist counselling and helping is whether and how to confront clients with issues of sexism. Helpers may also need to help women clients to anticipate and to deal with the consequences of changing their gender roles. One danger of bringing up issues of sexism too soon is that clients' resist the explanation and do not see its relevance. The opposite is also possible in that clients simplistically latch on to a sexist oppression analysis of their situations, get extremely angry with their partners, and prematurely leave them rather than attempt to work through their relationship issues.

The men's movement is the other, and sometimes missing half of the women's movement. There needs to be a greater development of men's helping to complement – and definitely not to compete against – responsible feminist helping. With some adaptation, the five central principles of feminist helping – egalitarian relationships, pluralism, working against oppression, external emphasis and valuing the experience of one's own sex – are highly relevant for men's counselling and helping too. Since women and girls easily outnumber men and boys as clients, probably many helpers and helping services need to become more user-friendly for males and skilled at working with the specific issues facing them.

As with multicultural counselling competencies, beginning helpers cannot be expected to learn everything at once. Gaining an initial awareness of how gender considerations can influence basic counselling skills, such as active listening and asking questions, is a good place to start in becoming genuinely gender-aware and sensitive helpers.

All helpers develop personal systems of ethics for how they work with clients. The word 'ethics' is sometimes defined as the science of morals in human conduct. Morals are concerned with the distinction between right and wrong and with accepted rules and standards of behaviour. Thus ethical codes or ethical guidelines for counselling and helping attempt to present acceptable standards for practice. Sometimes it is obvious when there has been an ethical lapse, for instance, engaging in sexual relations with clients. However, in the complexities of helping practice, ethical issues are often unclear. Consequently helpers are faced with ethical dilemmas involving choices about how best to act.

Ethical issues and dilemmas permeate helping practice. To use legal language, helpers always have a duty of care to their clients. Virtually everything helpers do can be performed ethically or unethically. Here I group ethical issues and dilemmas connected with enacting this duty of care into four main areas, albeit overlapping:

- helper competence;
- client autonomy;
- confidentiality; and
- client protection.

Helper competence

With so many approaches to helping, the issue arises as to what is competence. A useful distinction exists between relationship competence, offering a good helping relationship, and technical competence, the ability to assess clients and to deliver interventions. There is far greater agreement between the different helping approaches on the ingredients of relationship competence, such as respect and support for clients as persons and accurately listening to and understanding their worldviews, than there is for technical competence. Suffice it for now to say that technical competence is what leading practitioners in a given approach would agree to be competent performance of the technical aspects of that approach.

Another helpful distinction related to helper competence is that between readiness to practice and fitness to practice. Readiness to practice means that helpers require appropriate training and practice before they are ready to see clients and to use their counselling skills competently. Fitness to practice assumes that helpers have satisfactory counselling skills in their repertoires and it only becomes an ethical problem when they are precluded in some way from using these skills competently. An example of readiness to practice as an ethical problem is when helpers take on cases referred to them, for example anorexic clients, that are beyond their level of training and competence. An example of fitness to practice as an ethical problem is that of a counsellor who drinks at work and so fails to maintain competence.

Helpers can avoid ethical issues concerning readiness to practice if they are prepared to refer certain clients on to others more qualified to help them. Furthermore, where helpers do not possess the requisite competence to help some categories of clients, they can discourage colleagues from referring such people to them.

Helpers also have a responsibility to current and future clients to keep monitoring their performance and developing their counselling skills. Helpers always need to take care to evaluate and reflect upon what they do. In addition, where possible, it is desirable for helpers to receive either supervision or consultative support to gain insights into good skills and pinpoint other skills that they can improve.

Client autonomy

Respect for the client's right to make the choices that work best for them in their lives is the principle underlying client-self determination. Helpers should seek to support clients' control over and ability to assume personal responsibility for their lives. When, for example, helpers provide inaccurate pre-helping information or make false statements about their professional qualifications and competencies, they are stopping potential and actual clients from making informed choices about whether to commence and/or continue in helping with them.

Most often it is unnecessary and unrealistic for helpers to provide lengthy explanations to clients about what they do. Nevertheless, before and during helping, they can make accurate statements concerning the helping process and about their respective roles. Furthermore, helpers can answer clients' queries about helping honestly and with respect.

Helpers should also make realistic statements about the outcomes of helping and avoid making claims that might be disputed both outside and inside of law courts. Throughout helping, clients should be treated as intelligent participants who have a right to explanations about why helpers suggest strategies and what is entailed in implementing them.

An issue in client autonomy is where the values and backgrounds of clients may differ from those of their helpers, for instance, as a result of cultural or religious influences. Helpers should not impose their values on clients and, where appropriate, be prepared to refer clients on to other helpers who may more readily understand their concerns. It is highly unethical for helpers to assess and treat clients as pathological on the basis of judgements determined by culture, race, sex or sexual/affectionate orientation, among other characteristics.

Confidentiality

Sometimes it is said that all people have three lives: a public life, a private life and a secret life. Since helping frequently deals with material from clients' secret lives, their trust that their confidences will be kept is absolutely vital. However, there may be reasons connected with matters such as agency policy and sometimes the law, why helpers cannot guarantee confidentiality. For example, when helpers are working with minors – be it in private practice, educational or medical settings – there are many ethical and legal issues surrounding the boundaries of confidentiality and their obligations to parents, teachers and significant others.

Helpers should try to communicate pertinent limitations on confidentiality to clients in advance. Furthermore, other than in exceptional circumstances, helpers should seek clients' permission for any communication to third parties. Having said this, the issue of whether or not to disclose to third parties is at the forefront of ethical dilemmas for helpers, especially where risks to children are involved. In a study published in 1999 by British psychologists Geoff Lindsay and Petruska Clarkson, the answers of a sample of psychotherapists' reporting ethically troubling incidents concerning confidentiality fell into the following four areas:

- risk to third parties – sexual abuse;
- risk to the client – threatened suicide;
- disclosure of information to others – particularly to medical agencies, other colleagues, the client's close friends, relatives; and
- careless/inappropriate disclosure – by the psychotherapist or others.

Confidentiality assumes that clients have the right to control the disclosure of their personal information. In instances where helpers or helping students require tapes for supervision purposes, they should refrain from putting pressure on clients to be recorded. Most clients will understand a tactful request to record and, provided they are assured of the security of the tapes, will give their permission. In cases where clients have reservations, they are often reassured if told that they may stop the recording any time they wish.

Clients' records, whether they are case notes, cassettes or videotapes, need to be held securely at all times. A final word about confidentiality is that helpers, when talking socially with colleagues, relatives or friends, should learn to keep their mouths shut about details of their clients' problems and lives. Unfortunately, a few helpers are tempted to break confidentiality for the sake of a good story.

Client protection

The category of client protection encompasses looking after clients as persons. Helpers require sufficient detachment to act in clients' best interests. Dual relationships are those where, in addition to the helping relationship, helpers may already be in, or consider entering, or enter other kinds of relationships with clients: for instance, friend, lover, colleague, trainer and supervisor among others. As mentioned in Chapter 1, dual relationships are often part of the fabric of helping relationships where helpers perform other primary roles, for example nurse–patient. Therefore, whether a dual helper–client relationship is ethical, unethical or presents an ethical dilemma depends on the circumstances of the relationship.

Sexual contact with clients is always unethical. Instead of or as well as sexual exploitation, clients may also be subject to emotional and financial exploitation. Emotional exploitation can take many forms, but has the underlying theme of using clients in some way for helpers' personal agendas, for example, encouraging dependent and admiring clients rather than fostering autonomy. Financial exploitation can also take many forms including helpers charging for services they are unqualified to provide, overcharging and prolonging helping unnecessarily. Helpers also need to ensure that all reasonable precautions are taken to ensure clients' physical safety.

Helpers can protect clients and the public image of their professions if they take steps to address the detrimental behaviour of other helpers. Where they suspect misconduct by other helpers, they can be guided by their professional association's codes of ethics and practice. For instance, if a helper suspects misconduct by another helper, first they may be enjoined to resolve or remedy it through discussion with the helper concerned. If still dissatisfied, they can implement any complaints procedures provided by their professional association, doing so without breaches of confidentiality other than those being necessary for investigating the complaint.

27 Getting support and being supervised

Since many people who use basic counselling skills with clients may not have access to formal supervision arrangements, I divide this chapter into two overlapping parts: getting support and being supervised.

Getting support

There are many reasons why helpers may not have access to formal supervision arrangements to build their counselling skills. One reason is that many helpers are using counselling skills as part of other primary roles, for instance, teaching, nursing or offering financial advice. In such situations resources for staff support and development may focus on their primary tasks rather than on their counselling activities. Providing supervision to monitor and build employees' counselling skills can be expensive and time-consuming and employers may neither have nor perceive that they have sufficient funds for this purpose. Furthermore, some institutions and agencies attach a low priority to the use of counselling skills by their employees, instead preferring them to take more directive approaches.

In work and voluntary agency settings, apart from formal supervision, there are a number of ways in which helping students and helpers can gain valuable support and assistance in building their counselling skills. They may be assigned to bosses or mentors with whom they review their work on a regular basis or seek help when they feel they need it. They may also be part of teams that meet on a regular basis in staff meetings and case conferences to discuss how to deal with clients.

In such instances, helping students and helpers may have access to skilled team leaders who can both teach them how to improve their basic counselling skills and also draw on the experience of the other group members to provide enriched learning environments. In addition, work settings or voluntary agencies may run special workshops or short courses to assist helpers to develop specific skills for dealing with special clienteles. Furthermore, the settings in which helpers use counselling skills may have their own support systems of competent professionals with whom they can discuss individual clients.

In instances of inadequate provision of support from institutions and agencies, helping students and helpers can identify more experienced colleagues to act as informal mentors. In addition, they can consider forming their own peer support groups. On occasion, helpers may be forced to look outside their employing institutions or agencies to obtain suitable professional advice, for instance, from trusted counselling professionals or psychiatrists. However, in such instances, helpers need to be guided by the best interests of clients and be very sensitive to protecting their rights to confidentiality. In addition, as discussed in Chapter 15, where helpers and their mentors feel out of their depth, they often have the option of referring clients to those more suitably qualified. However, this is not always the case.

Being supervised

Helping students and helpers requires competent supervision to develop their counselling skills well. Supervision literally means overseeing. Helping students and helpers can discuss their use of counselling skills with experienced practitioners who can assist them to develop the effectiveness of their work with clients. A distinction exists between 'training supervision' and 'consultative supervision'. Training supervision is part of the ongoing training of helping students both on courses and when on probation. Consultative supervision is an egalitarian arrangement between one or more qualified helpers who meet together for the purposes of improving the practice of at least one of them. The major emphasis in the remainder of this chapter is on how to benefit from regular and systematic training supervision.

Goals and formats for supervision

The overriding goal of supervision is to assist those supervised to think and communicate as effective helpers and, in so doing, to become their own *internal* supervisors. Early on, supervisors may have to do some 'hand holding' as they assist beginning helpers in breaking the ice with real clients. In addition, students can receive help from their supervisors to assist them to examine and address poor mind skills contributing to performance anxiety. Throughout supervision, supervisees should receive emotional support in a way that encourages self-reliance and honest self-appraisal rather than dependence and a need for supervisor approval.

Supervisions can take place either one-to-one or with two or more helpers. Resources permitting, my preference, especially when helpers start seeing clients, is for individual supervision. Advantages of individual supervision include providing supervisees with adequate time to be supervised thoroughly and the fact that many supervisees are more likely to discuss sensitive issues regarding clients and themselves than if supervised with others.

Small group supervision also has some advantages. For example, members may get exposure to a greater range of clients and develop skills of discussing and receiving feedback on their work from peers as well as from their supervisor. Furthermore, supervisees can be more self-disclosing in the context of other supervisees' honest appraisals of their performance.

A combination of participating in individual supervision and in counselling skills training groups has much to recommend it. Supervisees can learn assessment skills and different helping strategies in training groups. Also, in such groups they can share their experiences of working with clients in ways that may be beneficial for all concerned.

To some extent the supervision process parallels the helping process, in that supervisors should develop good collaborative working relationships with students to provide fertile contexts in which to monitor and improve their skills. In supervision, however, the emphasis is on improving the mind skills and the communication skills required for effective helping rather than on managing personal problems. In a recent British study, both supervisees and supervisors rated creating a learning relationship as the most important of seven tasks of counselling supervision.

The supervision literature is full of references to counter-transference, the process by which helpers distort how they perceive and behave towards clients to meet their own needs. For instance, supervisees – and even experienced helpers too – may, at varying levels of awareness, be encouraging dependency, sexual interest or even distance in some clients. Effective supervision assists supervisees to identify, explore and address such distortions, at least insofar as they affect the their work with clients. Supervisors should also identify and address their own counter-transference distortions towards those whom they supervise.

Presenting material in supervision

The following are some methods whereby supervisees can present helping session content in supervision sessions. Some of these methods can be used in combination to add to the validity of understanding what actually transpired.

- *Verbal report* Verbal reporting on its own relies entirely on memory, which will certainly be incomplete and will almost certainly be highly selective. The greater the period of time between sessions and supervision, the more invalid memory may become. Furthermore, if supervisees are seeing other clients, it becomes difficult to remember exactly what happened with whom.
- *Process notes* Process notes, if written up immediately after helping sessions and using a structured format, do not rely so heavily on memory. Such notes can act as an aid to memory during supervisions. The combination of process notes and verbal report, while still open to a high degree of invalidity, is probably more valid than relying on verbal report alone.
- *Audiotaping* Audiotaping means that there is a valid record of all the verbal and vocal content of sessions. Another advantage of audiotaping is that either supervisees can choose or supervisors request specific segments on which to focus. Audiotaping can be relatively unobtrusive when only a small microphone is visible to clients.
- *Videotaping* Videotaping has the great advantage over audiotaping in that there is a valid record of bodily as well as verbal and vocal session content. Viewing videotapes of sessions is my preferred way of conducting supervisions. However, some placements may not be set up for videotaping, in which case audiotaping is the next best choice. A possible disadvantage of videotaping is that the machinery tends to be much more obtrusive than that required for audiotaping.
- *Role-playing* Where videotaping is not available, role-playing can provide a way of finding out how supervisees actually communicate with clients. The supervisee can orient the supervisor to the client's role and then counsel the supervisor as 'client' in a way that resembles part of the actual session.
- *Client feedback* Clients can provide feedback relevant to understanding what happened in helping sessions in a number of ways.

Supervisors and supervisees should take note of and try to understand the reasons for single session clients and for missed appointments. Towards the end of helping sessions, supervisees can ask their clients to provide feedback about the helping relationship and procedures. Clients can also fill out brief post-session questionnaires asking them for similar feedback.

Making use of supervision

Supervision sessions can be broken down into three phases: preparation, the supervision session itself and follow-up. In the preparation phase, supervisees can do such things as write up and reflect on their session notes and go through audiotapes or videotapes selecting excerpts for presentation of their use of good and poor counselling skills. In addition, they can read up on possible helping strategies to use with clients, think about issues connected with differences between themselves and their clients, ponder ethical issues, and in other ways reflect upon how they can make the most of their supervision time.

Early in sessions, supervisees and supervisors can establish session agendas. Sometimes, helpers only get one supervision hour for five or eight hours of client contact. If taping is used, important decisions can be which tapes to present and, for those tapes chosen, which excerpts to review. When observing videotapes, a risk is that so much time is spent watching the first few minutes of a session that later work in sessions either receives none or insufficient attention.

In Chapter 17, I mentioned the importance of helpers using client-centred coaching skills with clients. Supervisees may gain from similar skills being employed by their supervisors during their time together. Sometimes supervisors may wish to stop tapes to point something out. However, on many occasions, supervisees should be the ones to choose which excerpts to present and when to stop tapes for discussion. Supervisors can facilitate the process by asking questions such as 'What was going on there?', 'What were you trying to do?', 'What were you feeling?' and 'What skills were you using and how well were you using them?' Within the context of good collaborative working relationships, supervisors develop students' skills of thinking systematically about their helping work so that they may become their own internal supervisors. Towards the end of supervision sessions, both participants can review its main points and negotiate any specific homework assignments.

The follow-up phase of a supervision session has two main goals. One goal is that of supervisees using in their next sessions with clients the improved skills that they discussed and worked on in supervision.

Another goal is that of carrying out specific homework assignments. For instance, supervisee and supervisor may agree that the supervisee should practice a specific helping strategy before using it in a helping session. A further assignment might be reading some specific references relevant to particular clients' problems. Supervision homework can also focus on improving supervisees' mind skills and not just on those of their clients. For example, supervisees can agree to spend time challenging and restating any demanding rule or rules that contribute to their performance anxiety.

Supervisees vary in their ability to make the most out of supervision. Some are not prepared to work hard at achieving competence. Others have personal problems of such magnitude that possibly they should not be counselling clients at all until their own lives are in better shape. It is particularly hard to supervise students who are defensive and possess little insight into how their poor mind and communication skills interfere with their helping. Some supervisees are difficult to supervise because, in varying degrees, they know it all already. A minority of supervisees initiate and/or engage in unethical behaviour, be it with either their clients or their supervisors.

28 Becoming more skilled

Once helpers acquire some basic counselling skills, they are challenged to become even more skilled. However, they work in numerous contexts and roles, have widely disparate backgrounds and experience, and also differ in their motivation to improve their skills. Consequently, any suggestions for becoming more skilled need be taken in the context of individual helpers' evaluations of their current counselling skills and also of their personal agendas, work requirements and career aspirations.

Building skills

What are some of the methods helpers can use to maintain and develop their counselling skills? They can observe and listen to demonstrations by skilled counsellors and helpers. For instance, cassettes of interviews conducted by leading counsellors and psychotherapists are available for purchase in Britain and Australia. Also, helpers can purchase or hire videotapes. In Britain, films and videotapes may be hired from the British Association for Counselling and Psychotherapy (see Appendix 2). In addition, helpers may learn from written demonstrations of counselling skills. Transcripts of interviews by leading therapists are available, sometimes accompanying cassettes. Another way one can learn from demonstration is to become the client of a skilled helper, though this should not be the primary motivation for seeking counselling help. When a graduate student in counselling, I learned a considerable amount about how to establish collaborative working relationships from my 50 or so hours of individual therapy with a highly skilled client-centred counsellor.

While a whole interview approach to observing, listening to and reading transcripts is valuable, this is not the only way to approach the material. One option is to focus on smaller segments of interviews, say five minutes, and to look out for how specific counselling skills are used. In addition to verbal communication, helpers should focus on vocal messages and, if observing videos, on body messages as well.

Another option is to turn the audio or video recorder off after each client statement, form your own helper response, and then see how the helper actually responded. When working with transcripts of a session by someone like Carl Rogers, helpers can go down the page covering up Rogers' responses, form their own, and then check Rogers' responses. Their responses will not necessarily be inferior to those of the more famous helpers.

Co-counselling is a form of peer helping whereby in a given time period, say an hour, each person takes turns at being both helper and client. Helpers can practice counselling skills with colleagues on a co-counselling basis, using audio and video feedback where appropriate. In addition, they may be able either to form or become part of peer self-help groups in which the members work with, comment on and support one another as they develop their counselling skills.

Whether in informal helping contacts or in more formal helping sessions, many helpers already use counselling skills either as part of their jobs or in voluntary capacities. In some settings, they may be able to monitor themselves by recording and playing back sessions, possibly in the presence of supervisors or peers. In addition, they can be sensitive to feedback from clients. Some of this feedback will come in how clients respond with their verbal, vocal and body messages to helpers' use of counselling skills. In addition, where appropriate, helpers can ask clients for feedback on how they experienced individual sessions and about their overall helping contact with them. Helpers can also develop their own questionnaires, however brief, to generate client feedback.

Training paths

Where do helpers go next if they want to gain more training in counselling skills? Many readers may be in professions, for example social work or nursing, where there may be opportunities for further training either within their existing undergraduate or postgraduate courses or, if already graduated, on in-service training courses and workshops run by their professional association or by members of it. Other readers may work in voluntary organizations that offer their own intermediate or advanced counselling skills training courses geared to the populations that they serve.

Readers wishing to become counsellors or counselling psychologists should look out for accredited and/or well regarded courses. In Britain, the British Association for Counselling and Psychotherapy annually publishes *The Training in Counselling and Psychotherapy Directory*. In both Australia and Britain, the main route to becoming a counselling psychologist now is through undergraduate work in psychology followed by a Masters in Counselling Psychology. Those so inclined can contact the relevant counselling psychotherapy and psychology professional association for details of accredited courses (see Appendix 2).

Graduation from a counselling, psychotherapy or counselling psychology course does not in itself mean accreditation. To obtain accreditation, graduates will be required to accumulate a set number of hours of supervised helping practice. Afterwards, to maintain accreditation, helpers may be required to have ongoing supervision or regularly accumulate continuing professional development points by attending conferences, workshops and training courses.

A distinction exists between accreditation by a professional association and mandatory registration or licensing by either a national registration board or, as in Australia, by a state registration board. In some states in Australia people cannot call themselves counselling psychologists unless certified as such by the relevant state registration board. In both Britain and Australia, the trend is towards tightening up the licensing of counsellors, psychotherapists and counselling psychologists. The recent development of the United Kingdom Register of Counsellors is an important milestone on the British landscape.

Attending conferences, short courses and workshops can provide an informal training path whereby both beginning and more experienced helpers can improve their knowledge and skills. In Britain, details of short courses, workshops and conferences can be found in the British Association for Counselling and Psychotherapy's monthly *Counselling and Psychotherapy Journal* and in the British Psychological Society's monthly journal *The Psychologist*. Similar information is available in journals published by Australian psychology and counselling professional associations (see Appendix 2). Furthermore, in both countries information about short courses, workshops and conferences can be found in the newsletters and journals of other counselling-related professional associations, for instance those for human resource management, and of voluntary agencies such as *Relate News* in Britain.

If readers are interested in developing their counselling skills in a particular approach to helping, they can enquire whether there is a training centre in their locality. Most major helping approaches have international networks for training and practice. For example, agencies for specialized training in Person-Centred Therapy exist in Britain and for Rational Emotive Behaviour Therapy in both Britain and Australia.

Books and journals

Books

There is a large theoretical literature that underpins the use of counselling skills. This can be divided into primary sources, books and articles written by the leading theorists themselves, and secondary sources, books and articles written about the different theoretical approaches by people other than their originators. Ultimately, there is no substitute for reading primary sources. However, it can be a daunting task for the beginning helper to know where to start and how to cover the ground. In order to help readers to access the counselling and helping literature, I have provided a fairly extensive Annotated Bibliography as Appendix 1 of this book. The bibliography is divided into two main sections: counselling and helping practice and counselling and helping approaches.

Journals

Journals provide an excellent means of keeping abreast of the counselling skills literature. Some readers of this book are in fields such as nursing, social work and human resource management, whose professional journals may contain some articles about the use of counselling skills.

Box 28.1 provides a list of some of the main counselling and counselling psychology journals. Two of the journals – *Counselling and Psychotherapy Research* and the *Journal of Counseling Psychology* – focus mainly on research.

Box 28.1 Some leading counselling and counselling psychology journals

Counselling

Australian Journal of Guidance and Counselling

British Journal of Guidance and Counselling

Counselling and Psychotherapy Journal (British Association for Counselling and Psychotherapy)

Counselling and Psychotherapy Research (British Association for Counselling and Psychotherapy)

Journal of Counseling and Development (American Association for Counselling)

New Zealand Counselling and Guidance Association Journal

International Journal for the Advancement of Counselling

Counselling psychology

The Australian Counselling Psychologist (Australian Psychological Society)

Counselling Psychology Review (British Psychological Society)

Journal of Counseling Psychology (American Psychological Association)

The Counseling Psychologist (American Psychological Association)

Personal counselling and self-help

Personal counselling

Some helpers will have been clients before embarking on basic counselling skills training and may still be continuing in counselling. Reasons why helpers should consider undergoing therapy include personal growth, gaining empathic understanding of the client's position, and extending their experience of types of therapy.

Personal counselling can be very beneficial in working through blocks to being a happier, more fulfilled and humane person. In addition, helpers may address material in personal counselling related to their placements and supervisions, for instance, fears about dealing with certain kinds of clients and tendencies towards over-involvement or under-involvement. Either in addition to or instead of individual counselling, helpers wishing to deal with past deprivations and current problems can also consider undertaking couples, family or group modes of counselling. Furthermore, participating in lifeskills training groups, for instance focused on assertion skills or managing stress skills, can help some helpers to becoming stronger and more skilled human beings.

An issue in counsellor and helper training is whether undergoing personal counselling should be mandatory. Above I have presented some ways in which personal counselling might be beneficial. However, there is another side to the issue. Reservations about making personal counselling a criterion for the accreditation of counsellors and helpers include relevance, coercion, cost, defining the minimum length and insufficient research evidence. Regarding relevance, counselling approaches differ in the importance they attach to students undergoing personal counselling. Regarding coercion, counselling is not necessarily going to be effective when in response to a bureaucratic demand. Regarding cost, adding the costs of personal counselling to the expense of helper training leads to elitism and discriminates against poorer students. Regarding the required length of counselling, approaches differ on how long personal counselling should be and on whether it is necessary at all. Finally, regarding the research evidence for the effectiveness of personal counselling in enhancing helping practice, the case has still to be proven.

Self-help

Counselling skills training can provide students with the tools for improving their own functioning. When reflecting upon the experiences of their daily lives, students can treat themselves as clients. They are still the same persons in their everyday roles, for instance as partners or parents, as in their helping roles. Sometimes, self-help is best done systematically. For example, helpers can clear sufficient temporal, physical and psychological space within which to create a collaborative working relationship with themselves. Next they can clarify and expand their understanding of what is going on in problem situations. During this process they can identify unhelpful thoughts and communication/actions and translate these into specific mind skills and communication/action skills they wish to improve. Then, applying some of the helping strategies described in this book to themselves, they can work to improve their effectiveness.

As time goes by helpers are likely to get wise to characteristic poor mind skills and communication/action skills they employ. For example, a helper may develop skills at dissipating self-defeating anger through identifying, challenging and, if necessary, restating a demanding rule that was creating much of their anger. Helpers can also become adept at retrieving mistakes they make in their private lives by acknowledging them and using appropriate mind and communication skills to get back on track.

In addition to working on their own, helpers can be part of peer self-help groups and support networks. For example, members of women's groups, men's groups, gay and lesbian groups, and groups comprised of members of specific ethnic minorities can help one another to develop more of their humanity and to deal with personal, institutional and political oppression.

Appendix 1
Annotated bibliography

Counselling and helping practice

Bayne, R., Horton, I., Merry, T., Noyes, E. and McMahon, G. (1999) *The Counsellor's Handbook: A Practical A–Z Guide to Professional and Clinical Practice*. Cheltenham: Stanley Thornes.

This useful book consists of 200 or so descriptions of counselling concepts and skills in alphabetical order from A to Z. As an illustration of what to expect, the first ten entries under B are: Beginnings, Behaviour, Beliefs; irrational, Bereavement, 'Blocked' clients, Books; self-help, Boredom, Boundaries, Brainstorming and Brief counselling.

Bond, T. (2000) *Standards and Ethics for Counselling in Action*, 2nd edn. London: Sage.

This well-established textbook consists of four parts: The background, Responsibility to the client, The counsellor and others, and The whole picture. Highly recommended as an introduction to ethical issues and dilemmas in helping.

Burnard, P. (1999) *Counselling Skills for the Health Professions*, 3rd edn. Cheltenham: Stanley Thornes.

The 14 chapters of this book are focused on counselling in health contexts by such people as nurses, occupational therapists, physiotherapists, doctors and social workers. The book emphasizes such skills as attending and listening, questioning, reflecting, checking for understanding, helping with feelings and information. A good beginning text for those helpers either planning to work or working in medical settings.

Chaplin, J. (1999) *Feminist Counselling in Action*, 2nd edn. London: Sage.

This book presents a multi-stage rhythm model of feminist therapy. Chaplin illustrates each stage of the process with three case studies.

D'Ardenne, P., and Mahtani, A. (1999) *Transcultural Counselling in Action*, 2nd edn. London: Sage.

This book is written by two clinical psychologists, one with a white English and the other with an Indian background, working in London's East End. The book introduces the concept of transcultural counselling and then reviews practical issues concerned with clients, counsellors, starting the counselling process, sharing a common language, the therapeutic relationship, change and growth, and ending counselling. The book is illustrated by four case studies with clients of Bangladeshi, English, French and Nigerian cultural backgrounds.

Egan, G. (2001) *The Skilled Helper: A Problem-Management and Opportunity-Development Approach to Helping*, 7th edn. Pacific Grove, CA: Brooks/Cole.

Egan presents a three-stage, with three steps in each stage, problem-management and opportunity-development approach to effective helping. The book consists of six parts: Laying the groundwork, The therapeutic dialogue, Stage 1 of the helping model and advanced communication skills, Stage 2: helping clients determine what they need and want, Stage 3: helping clients develop strategies to accomplish their goals, and The action arrow: making it all happen. A separate publication is entitled *Exercises in Helping Skills: A Training Manual to Accompany the Skilled Helper*.

Feltham, C. and Horton, I. (eds) (2000) *Handbook of Counselling and Psychotherapy*. London: Sage.

This huge book of over 750 pages provides about 80 helpful introductory articles on a wide variety of issues. The book is divided into nine parts: Counselling and psychotherapy in context, Socio-cultural perspectives, Therapeutic skills and clinical practice, Professional issues, Theory and approaches, Client presenting problems, Specialisms and modalities, Tends and critiques, and Resources.

Milner, P. and Palmer, S. (eds) (2001) *Counselling: The BACP Counselling Reader*, Volume 2. London: Sage.

Published in association with the British Association for Counselling and Psychotherapy, this book is a companion to the 1996 *Reader*, Volume 1. Both books consist of articles from BACP's journal *Counselling* (renamed *Counselling and Psychotherapy Journal* in 2000). Over 90 articles in Volume 2 are divided into six parts, each with a separate introduction: Counselling approaches, Counselling contexts and practice, Counselling issues, Counselling and research, Future trends, and The last word.

Nelson-Jones, R. (2002) *Essential Counselling and Therapy Skills: The Skilled Client Model.* London: Sage.

This intermediate and advanced level textbook is based on the assumption that counsellors and therapists are only skilled to the extent that they can skill their clients. The book consists of three parts. Part one is an introductory chapter that addresses the question of what are essential counselling and therapy skills. Part two consists of 12 chapters describing each stage and phase of the author's skilled client model which stresses forming collaborative working relationships, assessing clients' good and poor skills, and intervening accordingly. Numerous interventions are described for changing clients' communications/actions, thinking, and feelings and physical reactions. Part three focuses on practice and training issues: namely diversity-sensitive counselling, ethical issues, and supervision and continuing professional development.

Palmer, S. and Laungani, P. (eds) (1999) *Counselling in a Multicultural Society.* London: Sage.

This many-authored British book contains eight chapters on such topics as the challenges of counselling in a multiracial society, culture and identity, racial issues, models of counselling and therapy for a multiethnic society, counselling needs of ethnic minorities, client centered or culture centered counselling, and the search for effective counselling across cultures.

Sue, D.W., Carter, R.T., Casas, J.M., Fouad, N.A., Ivey, A.E., Jensen, M., LaFromboise, T., Manese, J.E., Ponterotto, J.G. and Vazquez-Nutall, E. (1998) *Multicultural Counseling Competencies: Individual and Organizational Development.* London: Sage.

This American book introduces the concepts of multiculturalism and ethnocentric monoculturalism and then presents the multicultural counselling competencies. Chapters follow on understanding the Euro-American worldview and on understanding racial/ethnic minority worldviews. Much of the remainder of the book focuses on multicultural organizational development, with the final chapter looking at issues of personal, professional and organizational multicultural competence.

Counselling and helping approaches

Psychoanalysis

Freud, S. (1976) *The Interpretation of Dreams*. Harmondsworth: Penguin. Original edition 1900.

This book is Freud's major work. In it he reviews the scientific literature about dreams, demonstrates his method of interpreting dreams, and discusses dreams as fulfillments of wishes, distortion in dreams, the material and sources of dreams, dream-work, and the psychology of the dream process.

Freud, S. (1949) *An Outline of Psychoanalysis*. New York: W. W. Norton. Originally published posthumously in 1940.

Written just before Freud's death, this book provides an excellent concise introduction to psychoanalysis. The book consists of three parts: The mind and its workings, The practical task, and The theoretical yield.

Analytical therapy

Jung, C.G. (1968) *Analytical Psychology: Its Theory and Practice*. New York: Vintage Books.

This book presents the five lectures, plus discussion, that Jung gave at the Tavistock Clinic in London in 1935. Topics covered include the structure of the mind, word association and psychological types, and the methods of active imagination, dream analysis and the analysis of the transference. This book provides an excellent concise introduction to analytical psychology.

Jung, C.G. (1966) *The Practice of Psychotherapy* (2nd edn). London: Routledge (Volume 16 in *The Collected Works of C.G. Jung*)

This book is divided into two parts. Part one, entitled General problems of psychotherapy, contains nine papers, including one on the aims of psychotherapy. Part two, entitled Specific problems of psychotherapy, contains Jung's ideas on the therapeutic value of abreaction, the practical use of dream analysis, and the psychology of the transference.

Person-centred therapy

Rogers, C.R. (1961) *On Becoming a Person: A Therapist's View of Psychotherapy*. Boston: Houghton Miflin.

Regarded by Rogers as one of his most significant publications and certainly his most popular one. The book comprises seven parts: Speaking personally, How can I be of help?, The process of becoming a person, A philosophy of persons, The place of research in psychotherapy, What are the implications for living? and The behavioural sciences and the person.

Rogers, C. R. (1980) *A Way of Being*. Boston: Houghton Mifflin.

A collection of 15 papers written between 1960 and 1980, this book is divided into four parts: Personal experiences and perspectives, Aspects of a person-centred approach, The process of education – and its future, and Looking ahead – a person-centred scenario. This book is written in the same reader-friendly style as *On Becoming a Person*.

Mearns, D. and Thorne, B. (1999) *Person-Centred Counselling in Action*, 2nd edn. London Sage.

Engagingly written, this best-selling text introduces person-centred theory and practice in a way that clearly and sensitively brings to life the processes going on within and between counsellors and clients. The book's eight chapters are: The person-centred approach, The counsellor's use of the self, Empathy, Unconditonal positive regard, Congruence, 'Beginnings', 'Middles', and 'Endings'.

Gestalt therapy

Perls, F.S. (1973) *The Gestalt Approach & Eyewitness to Therapy*. New York: Bantam Books.

This book is a combination of two projects that Perls was working on at the time of his death. *The Gestalt Approach* is Perls' final statement of his theory. *Eyewitness to Therapy* provides descriptions of gestalt therapy in action.

Clarkson, P. (1999) *Gestalt Counselling in Action*, 2nd edn. London: Sage.

This book starts by introducing gestalt theory and the fundamentals of gestalt practice. A seven-stage cycle of gestalt formation and production is presented and, using the cycle as a framework, the practice of gestalt counselling is reviewed. This engaging and well-written book is a rich source of ideas about how to integrate experiments into gestalt practice.

Rational emotive behaviour therapy

Ellis, A., and Dryden. W. (1997) *The Practice of Rational Emotive Behaviour Therapy*. London: Free Association Books.

This book presents the general theory and basic practice of rational emotive behaviour therapy (REBT), with special chapters on how it is used in individual, couples, family, group, marathon and sex therapy. It brings Ellis's seminal 1962 book on REBT *Reason and Emotion in Psychotherapy* up to date and gives details of many REBT procedures.

Ellis, A. (2001) *Feeling Better, Getting Better, Staying Better: Profound Self-help Therapy for Your Emotions*. San Luis Obispo, CA: Impact Publishers.

A very detailed self-help book that provides a wide range of interventions for each of feeling better, getting better and staying better. This book goes beyond self-help to being a book that is extremely useful for helping students and practitioners wanting to learn about recent theoretical and practical developments in REBT.

Dryden, W. (1999) *Rational Emotive Behaviour Counselling in Action*, 2nd edn. London: Sage.

This introductory book succinctly and systematically presents the theory and practice of REBT. The book's three parts are: The basic principles of rational emotive behavioural counselling, The rational emotive behavioural counselling sequence, and The rational emotive behavioural counselling process.

Cognitive therapy

Beck, A.T., Rush, A.J., Shaw, B.F. and Emery, G. (1979) *Cognitive Therapy of Depression*. New York: John Wiley.

This book presents Beck's cognitive model of depression. The bulk of the book is a clinical handbook devoted to practical aspects of treating depressed clients, for instance, the therapeutic relationship, the application of both cognitive and behavioural interventions, and problems related to termination and relapse.

Padesky, C.A. and Greenberger, D. (1995) *Clinician's Guide to Mind Over Mood*; and Greenberger, D. and Padesky, C.A. (1995) *Mind Over Mood: Change How You Feel by Changing The Way You Think*. New York: Guilford Press.

These companion volumes are designed as step-by-step guides to the techniques and strategies of cognitive therapy. The manual is designed as a self-help workbook and the clinician's guide provides therapists with instructions on how to incorporate the workbook into individual and group psychotherapy.

Textbooks

Nelson-Jones, R. (2001) *Theory and Practice of Counselling & Therapy*, 3rd edn. London: Continuum.

This comprehensive textbook consists of 18 chapters: Creating counselling and therapy approaches, Freud's psychoanalysis, Jung's analytical therapy, Person-centred therapy, Gestalt therapy, Transactional analysis, Reality therapy, Existential therapy, Logotherapy, Behaviour therapy: Theory, Behaviour therapy: Practice, Rational emotive behaviour therapy, Cognitive therapy, Multimodal therapy, Cognitive-humanistic therapy, Cultural issues, Gender issues, and Evaluating counselling and therapy approaches. The Psychoanalysis, Analytical therapy, Person-centred therapy, Gestalt therapy, Rational emotive behaviour therapy and Cognitive therapy chapters have been extracted to form a shorter book called *Six Key Approaches to Counselling & Therapy*.

Palmer, S. (ed.) (2000) *Introduction to Counselling and Psychotherapy: The Essential Guide*. London: Sage.

Written mainly for beginning counsellors, counselling psychologists and psychotherapists in training, this edited book provides brief introductions to 23 different approaches to counselling and psychotherapy. The book's contents are intended to cover the main approaches currently practiced in Britain.

Appendix 2
Professional associations in Britain, Australia and America

Britain

British Association for Counselling and Psychotherapy
1 Regent Place
Rugby CV21 2PJ
Tel: 0870 443 5252
Fax: 0870 443 5160
Email: bacp@bacp.co.uk
Website: www.counselling.co.uk

British Psychological Society
St Andrews House
48 Princess Road East
Leicester LE1 7DR
Tel: 0116 254 9568
Fax: 0116 247 1787
Email: enquiry@bps.org.uk
Website: www.bps.org.uk

United Kingdom Council for Psychotherapy
167–169 Great Portland Street
London W1N 5FB
Tel: 020 7436 3002
Fax: 020 7436 3013
Email: ukcp@psychotherapy.org.uk
Website: www.psychotherapy.org.uk

Australia

Australian Psychological Society
PO Box 126
Carlton South
Melbourne
Victoria 3053
Tel: 03 9663 6166
Fax: 03 9663 6177
Email: naltoff@psychsociety.com.au
Website: www.aps.psychsociety.com.au

Psychotherapy and Counselling Federation of Australia
PO Box 481
Carlton South
Melbourne
Victoria 3053
Tel: 03 9639 8330
Fax: 03 9639 8340
Email: PACFA@bigpond.com
Website: www.pacfa.org.au

America

American Counseling Association
5999 Stevenson Avenue
Alexandria
VA 22304-3300
Tel: 703 823 8900 or 800 347 6647
Fax: 703 823 0252
Website: www.counseling.org

American Psychological Association
1200 17th Street, N.W.
Washington, DC 20036
Tel: 202 955 7600
Website: www.apa.org

Index

Introduction to Counselling Skills
Text and Activities

Richard Nelson-Jones
Director of the Cognitive Humanistic Institute, Chiang Mai, Thailand

'As a course book or an *aide* to individual learning this book contains a wealth of information and guidance based on years of study and practice. It is easy to use because it is clearly signposted. I particularly like the way the author addresses the range of issues a student needs to consider before embarking on a counselling course' – ***Counselling***

This practical and engaging textbook is for use on introductory courses aimed at developing fundamental counselling skills. Combining explanations, examples and activities, the book will be invaluable in a wide range of educational, voluntary and professional settings. Whether intending to work as counsellors or to use counselling skills in other professional roles, students will find this an essential source of information and guidance.

Abridged Contents

What Are Counselling Skills? \ Creating Your Mind \ Creating Your Communication and Feelings \ Helping as a Process \ Learning Counselling Skills \ Helping Relationships \ Improving Your Listening \ Starting the Helping Process \ Clarifying Understanding \ Expanding Understanding \ Setting Goals and Planning \ Strategies for Changing Communication and Actions \ Strategies for Changing Thinking \ Conducting Sessions and Ending Helping \ Introduction to Ethical Issues \ Becoming More Skilled and Human

1999 • 352 pages
Cloth (0-7619-6185-2) • Paper (0-7619-6186-0)

SAGE Publications Ltd, 6 Bonhill Street, London, EC2A 4PU, UK
order post-free **www.sagepub.co.uk**